Painting Animal Friends

The Nonconformist
Acrylic on Gessobord
10" x 8" (25cm x 20cm)

Painting
Animal Friends

JEANNE FILLER SCOTT

NORTH LIGHT BOOKS
CINCINNATI, OHIO
www.artistsnetwork.com

ACKNOWLEDGMENTS

I'd like to thank all of the animals who have posed for the paintings in this book. Many of these animals live or lived with me and my family. Cats include Peanut (Kitten), Hazel (Domestic Shorthair) and Marcie (Domestic Longhair); dogs, Katie (Dalmatian) and Laika (Mixed Breed); horses, Nelly (Draft Horse) and Moonlight (Shetland Pony); cows, Jessamine (Cow's Head) and Astrid (Calf); Casa and Blanca (Chicks—now two full grown white chickens!).

I'd also like to thank Anita and Leo Ackridge and their Holstein cow; Laurie Chatel and her Yorkshire terrier, Sindy; Harriet Fowler and her Lincoln Longwool sheep; the Pursleys and their golden retriever, Webster; Nancy Eaton and her thoroughbred horse, Vasari; and Janine Stubblefield and her Siamese cat, Sassy.

Also, I'd like to thank my editor, Vanessa Lyman, for her patience, encouragement and helpful suggestions.

Painting Animal Friends. Copyright © 2005 by Jeanne Filler Scott. Manufactured in China. All rights reserved. The patterns and drawings in this book are for personal use of the decorative painter. By permission of the author and the publisher, they may either be hand-traced or photocopied to make single copies, but under no circumstances may they be resold or republished. No other part of this book may be reproduced in any form or by any electronic or mechanical means including information storage and retrieval systems without permission in writing from the publisher, except by a reviewer who may quote brief passages in a review. Published by North Light Books, an imprint of F+W Publications, Inc., 4700 East Galbraith Road, Cincinnati, Ohio, 45236. (800) 289-0963. First Edition.

Other fine North Light Books are available from your local bookstore, art supply store or direct from the publisher.

09   08   07   06   05   5   4   3   2   1

Library of Congress Cataloging in Publication Data
Scott, Jeanne Filler.
   Painting animal friends/ Jeanne Filler Scott.— 1st ed.
      p. cm
   Includes index.
   ISBN 1-58180-598-5 (pb : alk. paper)
   1. Domestic animals in art. 2. Acrylic painting—Technique. I. Title.

ND1380.S377 2004
751.4'26—dc22   2004059530

Edited by Vanessa Lyman
Cover designed by Jenna Habig
Designed by Terri Eubanks
Production coordinated by Mark Griffin

F+W PUBLICATIONS, INC.

DEDICATION

I would like to dedicate this book to my two best art teachers:

Al Matzer, my high school art teacher, who recognized my talent, arranged for me to be in his class and taught me the basics of painting. An accomplished artist himself, Mr. Matzer valued traditional, realistic art at a time when most teachers were only interested in abstract art. He also encouraged me and my parents to send me to art school to pursue a career in art.

Joyce Sills, one of my art professors at Rutgers University, who also valued traditional art at a time when it was not "academically correct." Joyce, an accomplished artist who enjoys portraying elements of the natural world, inspired me with her strong sense of draftsmanship and composition.

METRIC CONVERSION CHART

To convert	to	multiply by
Inches	Centimeters	2.54
Centimeters	Inches	0.4
Feet	Centimeters	30.5
Centimeters	Feet	0.03
Yards	Meters	0.9
Meters	Yards	1.1
Sq. Inches	Sq. Centimeters	6.45
Sq. Centimeters	Sq. Inches	0.16
Sq. Feet	Sq. Meters	0.09
Sq. Meters	Sq. Feet	10.8
Sq. Yards	Sq. Meters	0.8
Sq. Meters	Sq. Yards	1.2
Pounds	Kilograms	0.45
Kilograms	Pounds	2.2
Ounces	Grams	28.3
Grams	Ounces	0.035

ABOUT THE AUTHOR

The animal art of Jeanne Filler Scott links painting techniques of the Old Masters with today's knowledge and appreciation of the natural world. When you look into the eyes of one of the animals featured in her paintings, you feel the animal looking back at you. "I paint with the understanding that each animal is unique," Jeanne says. "The animal may represent the entire species as an ideal, but on a deeper level, the animal before me is an individual. I try to do justice to my subjects and give their images the vitality and character they deserve."

An interviewer once wrote that the animals in Jeanne's paintings have the "spark of life," and this is certainly true. You immediately sense that her subjects are her intimate friends, and subtleties of their characters find expression in paint only because of long, sympathetic acquaintance.

That sense of life is what Jeanne imparts so well. The intelligent eyes of a wolf follow you around the room. A foal stands in a landscape of early morning mist, undecided whether to take a lump of sugar from your hand or break into a youthful gallop. In a peaceful wood, you relax with a red fox as he indulges in a satisfying stretch and contented yawn. Jeanne's paintings are celebrations of life.

Jeanne's work has appeared in many exhibitions, including the Society of Animal Artists, Southeastern Wildlife Exposition, National Wildlife Art Show, MasterWorks in Miniature, NatureWorks, Nature Interpreted (Cincinnati Zoo), American Academy of Equine Art, the

Jeanne and Leo

Kentucky Horse Park and the Brookfield Zoo. Several of her paintings are published as limited edition prints, a number of which are sold out.

Jeanne's paintings are published on greeting cards by Leanin' Tree, and she has been featured on the covers and in articles of magazines such as *Equine Images, Wildlife Art News, InformArt* and *Chronicle of the Horse.* She is the author of the book *Wildlife Painting Basics: Small Animals* (North Light Books 2002), and her work has been included in the books *The Best of Wildlife Art* (North Light Books 1997), *Keys to Painting Fur & Feathers* (North Light Books 1999) and *The Day of the Dinosaur* (Bison Books 1978), which was later re-released as *The Natural*

History of the Dinosaur. She is a member of the Society of Animal Artists and the Lexington Art League.

Jeanne and her family live on a farm in Washington County, Kentucky, surrounded by woods, fields and the Beech Fork River. Many kinds of wild creatures inhabit the farm, including opossums, deer, turkeys, raccoons, foxes, coyotes, box turtles, squirrels, woodchucks and rabbits. Jeanne, her husband Tim and son Nathaniel often rescue animals in need. Their animal family includes ten dogs, ten cats, eight chickens, two iguanas, seven horses, several cows, two rabbits and four opossums.

See more of Jeanne's work on her website at **www.jfsstudio.com.**

TABLE OF CONTENTS

INTRODUCTION

Painting Animal Friends will teach you how to paint domestic animals. These animals truly are our companions, as they've been with us for thousands of years. They've lived with people for so long that they're quite different from their wild ancestors. In return for our care, they give us such things as companionship, food, clothing and the opportunity to enjoy their beauty, their personalities and their characters.

I've included a variety of animals in this book, from cats and dogs to horses and other farm animals. You'll learn to paint them realistically, so that they look alive and breathing. Techniques for painting fur, wool, feathers, horse coats, manes and tails, expressive eyes, whiskers and different kinds of backgrounds are taught in the following demonstrations.

I encourage you to practice drawing animals, both from photos and from life. Template drawings are included so you can use them if you choose. If your drawing skills need some polishing, study the template drawings to see what essential lines you need when doing a sketch.

Above all, I hope you enjoy and learn from painting the animals in this book.

Painted Lady
Acrylic on panel
13" x 20" (33cm x 51cm)

MATERIALS NEEDED

All the paintings in this book are rendered in acrylic. The following pages contain information on materials and tips for working with acrylic.

BRUSHES

The brushes used in this book are: no. 0 round, no. 1 round, no. 2 round, no. 3 round, no. 4 round, no. 5 round, no. 6 round, no. 7 round, no. 8 shader and no. 10 shader. All of these brushes are either sable or synthetic sable, as I find that these work best for my detailed, realistic style of painting. I prefer the synthetic fiber brushes since they're both durable and less expensive than real animal hair, and I feel better knowing that no animal was harmed in manufacturing them.

Rounds are best for detail, as they come to a fine point. Although you will need some of the smaller rounds, such as no. 0 and no. 1, for very thin lines such as whiskers, in general, it is best to use a larger brush, such as a no. 3 or no. 5, because they come to a fine point and will hold more paint than a smaller brush. This saves you from having to dip your brush in the paint as many times before you finish a section.

Shaders, flats and filberts are good for painting broader areas. Since filberts are tapered, they can be more easily manipulated around contours.

It is best to have two to three of each type of the more frequently used brushes, such as nos. 3, 5 and 7 rounds. As you'll see in the demos, often you will need two or three of the same size brush, each for a different color, so you can use them alternately while blending.

SURFACE

The painting surface for the demonstrations in this book is Gessobord (a product of Ampersand Art Supply, Austin, TX), a preprimed Masonite panel with a nice texture for realistic painting. It comes in a variety of sizes. Most of the demos in this book were done on 8" x 10" (20cm x 25cm) panels, while a few were 9" x 12" (23cm x 30cm). For a couple of them—the cow's head and the baby chicks—I only used part of a panel.

JAR OF WATER

Water is the only medium I use to thin my acrylic paints. It is important not to let your water get too murky with paint.

PAPER TOWELS

Paper towels are used for blotting excess paint or water from your brush. Keep a folded paper towel by your palette and a crumpled one in your lap or hand.

NO. 2 PENCIL AND KNEADED ERASER

You'll need a pencil and an eraser for drawing or tracing the image onto your panel. The kneaded eraser is good for making corrections, or for lightening pencil lines on your panel so they won't show through the paint.

TRACING PAPER

Tracing paper is used to trace your sketch, or the template drawing provided with each demo, whichever you prefer. After tracing your sketch, you can transfer it to your Gessobord panel. The advantage of doing the sketch on a separate piece of paper, and not directly onto the panel, is that you have much more control over the size and the placement of your subject. This will usually result in a better painting.

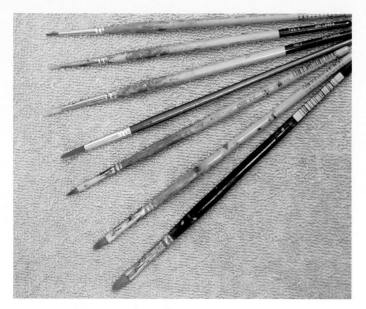

Brushes
A good selection of brushes for painting animals and backgrounds.

PALETTE

The Masterson Sta-Wet palette is very helpful, as it keeps your paints from drying out for days or even weeks. The 12" x 16" (30cm x 41cm) size is best, as it gives you plenty of room to mix colors. There is nothing more frustrating than to run out of room on your palette in the middle of a painting! The palette consists of a plastic box that is $1^3/_4$" (4cm) deep, and comes with a sponge insert that fills the bottom of the box when wet. A special disposable paper called Acrylic Film, which is discarded after it is used up, sits on top of the sponge insert. The box has an airtight lid.

The directions that come with this palette tell you to saturate the sponge with water and explicitly instruct not to wring out the sponge. However, I found that if I didn't press out some of the water, my paints turned into a soupy mess after a short time. If the paints start to dry after a few days, you can spray them lightly with water from a spray bottle.

PALETTE KNIFE

You'll need a palette knife for mixing colors. A tapered steel knife works best, and the trowel type (rather than straight) where the handle is lifted above the blade, is the easiest to use. Be sure to clean your palette knife between colors. Wiping it on a paper towel is usually sufficient, but you'll have to rinse it in your water jar occasionally.

WAX PAPER

There will be times when you need a color to be thicker than it is when on the surface of the Sta-Wet palette, as the palette always adds a small amount of water to the paint. For example, when painting a highlight that you really want to stand out, you want very little water mixed with the paint. It's useful to keep wax paper on hand so you can transfer some color to it if necessary. The paint will dry up quickly, but it will be a thicker consistency.

Palette
The Masterson Sta-Wet palette keeps your paints from drying out as you work. The tapered trowel-type palette knife is used for mixing colors.

Burnt
Sienna

Burnt
Umber

Cadmium
Orange

Cadmium
Red
Medium

Cadmium
Yellow Light

Payne's
Gray

Permanent
Hooker's
Green

Raw
Sienna

Scarlet
Red

Titanium
White

Ultramarine
Blue

Viridian

Yellow
Oxide

MIXING COLORS

The demos in this book were painted with Liquitex acrylic paints that come in tubes. I tried another brand recently, and while the paint itself was fine, the cap on the tube was so small that it couldn't be closed properly. I frequently found that the paint had dried out at the opening, which made it difficult to squeeze anything out. I've since switched back to Liquitex.

The colors used in the different demos vary with the subject, some requiring more colors than others. A complete list of the colors used in this book is: Burnt Sienna, Burnt Umber, Cadmium Orange, Cadmium Red Medium, Cadmium Yellow Light, Payne's Gray, Permanent Hooker's Green, Raw Sienna, Scarlet Red, Titanium White, Ultramarine Blue, Viridian and Yellow Oxide.

MIXTURES

Most of the colors you use will be a mixture of two or more paints. If you use colors straight from the tube, the result will probably be garish and unrealistic.

Be sure to mix a large enough quantity of each color or so that you have enough to finish the painting. This is easier than mixing the same color again. Save all of your color mixtures until you have completed the painting. You never know when you may need the color again to re-establish a detail, for example. You can also frequently use a previously mixed color as the basis for a new color. Simply add another color or two to a portion of a mixture you've already created.

TIP

When you mix a color on your palette, you can't be certain how it will look in the painting until you see it next to the colors already on your panel. Test the mixture by placing a small dab on the area to be painted. You can then modify the color so it will be the best for your painting.

Useful Acrylic Mixtures

Here are some useful color mixtures:

Black. Mix black for an animal's coat with Burnt Umber and Ultramarine Blue. This black looks more natural than black from a tube.

Warm White. Mix a warm white for animal fur, clouds, wildflowers, etc. with Titanium White and a touch of Cadmium Yellow Light or Yellow Oxide.

Basic Green. Mix a basic green for grass and trees with either Viridian (a cool green useful for evergreens and water reflections) or Permanent Hooker's Green (a warmer green useful for sunlit fields). Add small amounts of Cadmium Orange and Burnt Umber to tone down the green. For darker shadows, mix in some Ultramarine Blue and more Burnt Umber. For highlight colors, add some Titanium White and Yellow Oxide, Titanium White or Cadmium Yellow Light.

Natural Pink. Mix a natural pink for the noses and inside the ears of white-furred animals with Cadmium Red Medium, Yellow Oxide and a touch of Raw Sienna.

Basic Grass Color. Mix a basic grass color with Permanent Hooker's Green, Titanium White, Yellow Oxide and a small amount of Cadmium Orange.

Bluish Green. Mix a bluish green for distant trees with Titanium White, Permanent Hooker's Green, Ultramarine Blue and a bit of both Cadmium Orange and Raw Sienna.

Blue Sky Color. Mix a blue sky color with Titanium White, Ultramarine Blue and a touch of Yellow Oxide.

You can lighten or darken any of these colors to suit your painting. Experiment with these mixtures.

Black

warm white with
Cadmium Yellow
Light

warm white with
Yellow Oxide

basic green with
Viridian

basic green with
Permanent Hooker's
Green

natural pink

basic grass color

bluish green

blue sky color

BEGINNING A PAINTING

Template drawings of each animal are provided with each demonstration in this book. You can use these templates or create your own sketch.

TRANSFERRING YOUR SKETCH

Whether you use the template or a sketch of your own, use a piece of tracing paper and a fine point black marker to trace the image.

You can enlarge or reduce the size of the image to fit your panel with a copy machine or an opaque projector. If you use a photocopy, blacken the back of the copy with a no. 2 pencil, then tape it to your panel and trace with a pencil. You'll need to bear down with a fair amount of pressure, but this should result in transferring the graphite from the back of your photocopy onto the panel. Lift the tracing paper occasionally to make sure you are pressing down hard enough and are getting the complete image. If your tracing comes out too dark (so that it will show through the paint) use a kneaded eraser to lighten it.

If you use an opaque projector, you can trace the sketch directly onto the panel from the projected image. This is a little more difficult than you might think, since you have to stand to one side so you don't block the light from the projector.

DOING AN UNDERPAINTING

Once you have a pencil sketch on your panel, you are ready to do the underpainting. Neutral colors such as Burnt Umber or Payne's Gray, thinned with water, are good for this. As a rule of thumb, use Burnt Umber for brown or warm-colored animals—such as a chestnut horse—and Payne's Gray for gray, black, or white animals, such as a Dalmatian.

Squeeze out some of the underpainting color onto your palette, then mix it with a small amount of the water on the palette's surface. You want the paint to be thin but not too runny. Begin to paint, not worrying much about detail at this point. Just establish the main lines and the lights and darks. The purpose of the underpainting is to give you a rough guide to go by when you begin painting in full color.

The Sketch
With homemade carbon paper positioned underneath, the sketch is ready to be traced onto the panel.

TIP

You can make your own carbon paper by blackening the back of a blank piece of tracing paper with a no. 2 pencil. You can use this homemade carbon paper over and over.

GENERAL STEPS FOR COMPLETING THE PAINTING

Once you have finished the underpainting, you are ready to apply the darkest value colors. This is followed by the middle value and then the lightest value colors. You will start with a small amount of detail, building upon this and adding more detail with each step. Doing a realistic painting is basically a process of refining as you go along and building upon what you've already done. In the final step, you will paint the finishing details.

THICKNESS OF THE PAINT

When painting with acrylics, use just enough water so that the paint flows easily. You will usually need to apply two to three layers to cover an area adequately. Since the paint dries so quickly, this is easily accomplished. In general, shadows are painted fairly thin, while highlighted areas benefit from a little more thickness, which makes them stand out.

TYPES OF BRUSHSTROKES

Learning to handle your brush is crucial in depicting the texture of fur, clouds, grass and hooves. There are several types of strokes you should be familiar with when painting the natural world.

Dabbing Vertical Strokes

These strokes are done quickly, in a vertical motion, with either a round or a flat brush. They are good for painting the texture of grass in a field.

Smooth Flowing Strokes

These strokes are good for long hair, such as a horse's mane or a long-haired cat's tail. Use a round brush with enough water so the paint flows, and make the strokes flowing and slightly wavy.

Dabbing Semi-Circular Strokes

These are done fairly quickly, in a semi-circular movement, with a flat brush such as a shader. These strokes are good for skies, portrait backgrounds or other large areas that need to look fairly smooth, but not vertical or horizontal, such as a wall or floor.

Small Parallel Strokes

Use this kind of stroke to paint detail, such as short animal fur, using the tip of your round brush. Be sure to paint in the direction the hair grows on the animal.

Glazing

A glaze or wash is used to modify an existing color by painting over it with a different color thinned with water, so that the original color shows through. This creates a new color that you couldn't have achieved any other way. Dip your brush in water, then swish it around in a small amount of the glazing color. Blot briefly on a paper towel so you have a controllable amount of the glaze on your brush, then paint the color smoothly over the original color. In this example, a glaze of Burnt Sienna was painted over a portion of the log to show how the glaze warms up the colors.

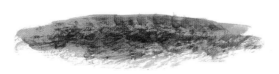

Drybrush or Scumbling

This is when you modify a color you've already painted by painting over it with another color in an opaque fashion, so that the first color shows through. Using a moist, not wet, brush, dip the brush into the paint, then rub it lightly on a paper towel, so that there is just enough paint to create a broken, uneven effect when you paint over the original color. Repeat as necessary.

Smooth Horizontal or Vertical Strokes

These strokes are good for man-made objects and water reflections. Using enough water so the paint flows, but is not runny, move your round brush evenly across the surface of the panel.

CREATING BACKGROUNDS

Your background is frequently as important as the animal itself. Don't forget to include some of your subject's natural setting.

Work on the background and the subject simultaneously. This will make it much easier to integrate the animal with its surroundings. In a painting where the subject is defined by the background colors, such as white ducks against dark water, you will need to paint the background color earlier in the process.

There are two types of backgrounds used in the demos in this book: portrait and full (landscape) backgrounds.

PORTRAIT BACKGROUND

A portrait background usually consists of a basic color that sets off the main subject. There is often some variation, such as darker versions of the color in some areas that are blended into the main color. Another variation can be achieved by drybrushing another color over the original color. If the entire body of the animal is shown, it's a good idea to paint a shadow or a few sprigs of grass around the subject. A portrait background is often used when a detailed background would distract from the subject, such as when painting a head portrait.

LANDSCAPE BACKGROUND

Landscape backgrounds are more of a challenge, but they can add a lot to a painting. The landscape does not need to have a lot of detail to be effective. In fact, having too much detail in the background will distract the viewer from the focal point. Paint just enough detail to make the background look realistic.

Close-up Grass

Paint close-up grass with a dark green shadow color and a lighter, basic grass color. Use round brushes to paint flowing, slightly curving strokes that taper at the ends and go in various directions. Overlap the greens and add some brown detail to integrate the animal and/or add realism, since most grass does not look as perfect as a golf course!

Clouds

Paint clouds in the sky with a warm white mixture. Use a flat brush and light, feathery dabbing strokes to paint the clouds right over the blue sky. Use a separate brush and the blue sky color to blend the undersides of the clouds with the sky.

Painting Trees

Paint trees with a basic green color mixture, using dabbing strokes and a flat brush. With a lighter green and a round brush, paint some detail to suggest clumps of leaves.

Broad Areas of Grass

Paint broad areas of grass with a combination of vertical and horizontal brushstrokes, with mostly vertical strokes in the foreground, transitioning to more horizontal strokes farther back. Make the strokes smaller as they recede into the landscape.

Skies

Paint skies with dabbing, semicircular strokes and a flat brush, such as a no. 10 shader. Make the sky lighter at the horizon by adding more Titanium White to a portion of the basic sky color, blending where the two colors meet.

FINDING ANIMAL SUBJECTS

There are many places where you can find domestic animals to sketch and photograph.

DOGS

Dog shows are a fascinating place to see a great variety of pure-bred dogs. You can see rare breeds such as Bouvier des Flandres and Nova Scotia Duck-tolling Retrievers, as well as plenty of examples of the better known breeds. Most of the owners are happy to let you photograph their dogs, as long as you don't use a flash, which might upset the dogs, or interfere in their busy dog show schedule. The American Kennel Club recognizes a large number of breeds, but there are some you won't see at an AKC show. Other kennel clubs, such as the United Kennel Club, recognize additional breeds such as the English shepherd and toy fox terrier. There are also breeds that have never been recognized by a major kennel club.

Humane societies always have many dogs needing homes. There you will see a great variety of mixed breed dogs, as well as purebreds. Humane society workers are usually friendly and will allow you to observe and photograph the dogs, especially if you can make a donation or volunteer some help. If you can adopt a dog, that would be even better!

Private dog owners are usually quite friendly and proud of their dogs. If you ask, they most often will be quite happy to allow you to photograph their dog.

Some of the dogs in this book are my own—my family has ten dogs, all rescued, some purebred and some mixed breed. Others were dogs whose portraits I was commissioned to paint or dogs I saw at various places.

CATS

Although I have never attended a cat show, I'm sure there would be a large variety of breeds represented. Most of the cats I've painted have been my own—at present, there are ten cats living in the house, all rescued over the years—or friends' or relatives' cats.

If you are looking for a particular breed or color cat, you can ask your local veterinarian for help. He or she will know many cat owners who can be approached. Of course, humane societies usually have cats needing homes also.

HORSES

There are many places to see horses—horse shows, race tracks, horse farms and state and county fairs. There are many types of horse shows, from shows that feature only one breed to shows that judge the performance of horses and riders. Most race tracks are for either Thoroughbred or Standardbred horses. Although you'll probably want to see the horses in the show ring or in a race, it is also very interesting to go behind the scenes where the horses are stabled.

State and county fairs and farm shows usually feature a variety of horses, from ponies to Arabians to draft horses. There are plenty of opportunities to observe, sketch and photograph them.

Horse farms are a great resource for mares and foals of different breeds. While some farms are open to visitors, you will need to ask permission to visit others. Of course, sometimes you can just pull off alongside the road and get some wonderful references.

Some larger cities have mounted police and carriage horses that would make very nice painting subjects.

Some of the horses in the demos belong to my family—all pets—while others I saw at horse farms or were subjects of portrait commissions.

COWS AND OTHER FARM ANIMALS

One of the best places to see a variety of farm animals is at a state or county fair or a livestock show. There you will see many examples of different breeds of cattle, sheep, goats, pigs, rabbits, chickens, ducks and other animals.

Breeding farms, animal rescue centers and private owners are other resources. There are many different ways of finding out about these places, but word of mouth is one of the best. Often, for example, the owner of a dog I am photographing will tell me about someone who has a private zoo. Other sources of information are friends and fellow artists. You can also do an Internet search to find all sorts of places you didn't know about where you can go to observe different kinds of animals.

Borrowing From Strangers

Several years ago, I had an exhibit at an outdoor art show in Lexington, Kentucky. This handsome white standard poodle and his owner stopped by to look at my artwork. With the owner's permission, I took a few photos of the dog, thinking that I would someday like to paint his portrait.

Standard Poodle
Acrylic on Gessobord
8" x 10" (20cm x 25cm)

Borrowing From Neighbors

This Lincoln Longwool sheep belonged to my neighbor in Jessamine County, Kentucky. Longwools are large sheep known for their abundant wool, which is used to weave carpets and blankets and is a lot of fun to paint.

Lincoln Longwool
Acrylic on Gessobord
8" x 10" (20cm x 25cm)

GATHERING REFERENCES

There are numerous ways to "collect" your references, but photography and sketching are probably the most common.

PHOTOGRAPHY

If you are serious about being an artist who paints animals in a realistic, detailed style, photography is an important tool. Since animals move constantly, getting good photos is a challenge. While you can only capture a few lines in a sketch, photographs can preserve a moment in great detail. This gives you a lot more information to work from and more flexibility as an artist.

CAMERA EQUIPMENT YOU'LL NEED

For basic photography, you'll need a 35mm camera with a normal lens and a telephoto zoom lens. The zoom lens is the most important because it allows you to take close-ups of distant animals. The zoom feature allows you to choose how you want to frame your subject. Even tame, domestic animals can be quite uncooperative about staying close by when you want to photo-

graph them! The normal lens is good for photographing animals that you can get very close to, as well as for taking background photos.

I generally use ASA 400 print film, as this film speed allows you to take photographs in fairly low light conditions. Also, a telephoto lens needs more light to operate, so the 400 speed gives you more latitude. For sunny days, ASA 200 film is good.

Make sure any camera you purchase has a motor drive (most do) so that you don't need to advance the film after each shot. If you're shopping for a camera, also consider purchasing a polarizing filter. These fit over the lens to cut down on haze and reflections.

TIPS FOR PHOTOGRAPHING ANIMALS

There is more to photographing animals than simply pointing the camera and pressing the shutter release. Here are some tips:

Get down to the animal's level. Inexperienced photographers often take photos of animals while looking down at them. In most cases, it is better to look at the animal straight on. Sometimes this means you will have to spend a lot of time in an uncomfortable position, crouching or even lying on the ground to photograph smaller animals, but the results are worth it!

Take several rolls of film. The more pictures you take, the greater the chance that you will get that one winning pose that is the basis for a great painting.

Take some close-ups of the animals' features. Photos of eyes, noses, feet, etc. can be extremely helpful when you are working on a painting and the animal is no longer in front of you. Often, the smaller details don't show up well in photos of the entire animal.

Have someone with you for assistance. Often, my husband or my son accompanies me to a photo session. Since they are very experienced with animals, they are real assets. One of the most common problems I have in photographing friendly animals like horses and dogs is that they insist on walking right up to my camera and sniffing the lens! Another person can distract the animal so it will look in another direction rather than right at the photographer.

Make sounds or motions that attract the animal's attention. When I am photographing a dog that looks bored and refuses to put its ears up, I often imitate a cat's meow. This usually caus-

The Basic Camera Equipment

A 35mm camera with a telephoto zoom lens and appropriate film are all you need to get started photographing animals.

es the dog to prick its ears and cock its head. But some animals just aren't that easily impressed! Sometimes, tossing a small twig or a handful of grass will cause an animal to momentarily look alert.

TAKING BACKGROUND PHOTOS

In the excitement of photographing the animal, don't forget to photograph the animal's environment if the location is appropriate for a painting. Later on, when you are in your studio working on a painting, you'll be glad you stopped to take a few photos of the background. Also, take close-up photos of elements you might like to include, such as wildflowers, grass, rocks, etc.

You can combine elements from different photos for use in a painting. When using more than one photograph—and when you have a strong light source in your main reference photo—be sure that you paint the background so that all light is coming from the same direction. If all of your photos were taken on a bright overcast day (which is the lighting preferred by many photographers), you don't have to worry about the light source.

FILING YOUR PHOTOS

It is important to keep your photos in files so that you can find them when you need them. The more specific you make your files, the more useful they will be to you. For example, I have hundreds of photos of horses. Some of my file headings are: Foals, Standing; Foals, Heads; Mares and Foals, Paint; Mares and Foals, Thoroughbred, Grazing.

SKETCHING

Sketching is a great way to observe animals and have fun at the same time. While you'll discover that animals seldom hold a pose for more than a few moments or seconds, even while they are at rest, you'll learn a lot about their anatomy and their character. Always carry your sketchbook so you can take advantage of opportunities—you never know when you might see an interesting animal, tree or other natural object. You'll enjoy looking at your sketchbooks later to see what you have captured and to remember the experience.

BOOKS

Well-illustrated books about animals are a good source of information. I have a large collection of animal books that I refer to on a regular basis—animal encyclopedias, nature field guides and books on animals in art. I've purchased many of these books at used bookstores and library book sales, where you can buy books for a fraction of what they cost new. Children's books usually have good pictures, and you can find books that specialize in a particular animal or group of animals, such as pigs or farm animals, that you might not find in books written for adults.

FOUND OBJECTS

Found objects are natural things that add interest to your paintings, such as wildflowers, fallen logs or an ear of corn. You can bring such objects into your studio and incorporate them into your paintings. Set them up so the lighting is the same as in your reference photo.

Sketching

Sketching an animal trains your artistic eye, but it also helps you get to know your subject.

I

Cats

Our animal family currently includes ten cats, none of whom we actually planned to acquire! Our oldest cat, Hazel, simply showed up at our back door one day. Aslan, Otsu and Tamika, a brother and two sisters, were tiny orphaned kittens living in a patch of weeds next to a busy road. We caught them, one by one, with a live trap we borrowed from the local humane society. We found Isis, a beautiful black cat, abandoned with her four littermates along a wooded country road not far from our farm. Since we already had nine cats, we kept Isis and found good homes for the other kittens. We picked up Leo, a black-and-white cat with long, silky hair, and Sabrina, a pretty gray tabby with golden eyes, as half-grown kittens along roads in our area. When we lived in Texas, my son, Nathaniel, found our other gray tabby, Sherpa, when she was a tiny kitten; she was wandering in and out of cages where stray dogs were held by the county. Delta, a young gray cat with white markings, showed up thin and hungry on our Kentucky farm one winter. She is now quite plump! Hester, a long-haired gray cat, lived in the crawl space beneath a restaurant. She was skinny and her hair full of tangles. Today, she is a pretty cat who keeps herself very well groomed. I have enjoyed not only helping these cats, but getting to know them as distinct personalities.

Marcie
Acrylic on Gessobord
12" x 9" (30cm x 23cm)

DOMESTIC SHORTHAIR

PAINT COLORS

 Payne's Gray

 Burnt Umber

 Ultramarine Blue

 Burnt Sienna

 Cadmium Orange

 Permanent Hooker's Green

Titanium White

 Raw Sienna

 Scarlet Red

 Yellow Oxide

 Cadmium Yellow Light

MIXTURES

 black

 bluish shadow

 ginger color

 warm shadow

 pink

 yellowish eye color

 detail for black

 shadow between the front legs

 grayish color

 detail black part of the tail

 nose and muzzle

 dark green

 weathered gray

REFERENCE

Hazel showed up at our door fifteen years ago, apparently homeless. We fed her and she stayed. Two years later, one of our neighbors spotted the cat and told me that Hazel used to be their cat. The neighbor said they had decided to make Hazel an outdoor cat, so she must have gone shopping for a new home! I guess she likes us, as she has never left. Hazel is spending her old age as a pampered indoor cat.

STEP 1: Establish the Form and the Dark Values

Lightly draw the cat and fence post in pencil. Use a kneaded eraser to lighten any lines that come out too dark. With a no. 5 round and Payne's Gray thinned with water, establish the main lights and darks. For broad areas, use a no. 7 round.

For the black coat color, mix Burnt Umber and Ultramarine Blue. With a no. 3 round, paint the black parts of the cat's coat. Use a no. 1 round for the outline of the eyes. As the paint dries, add more layers until the dark areas are dense.

BRUSHES

Nos. 0, 1, 3, 4, 5 and 7 rounds

No. 10 shader

"For the background, I mixed a dark green with Permanent Hooker's Green, Burnt Umber, Cadmium Orange and Ultramarine Blue. I painted with a no. 10 shader, using a no. 4 round to paint around the cat's outline."

"For the weathered gray fence post, I mixed together Titanium White, Ultramarine Blue, Burnt Sienna and Burnt Umber. I painted the fence post with vertical strokes."

STEP 2: **Paint the Middle Value Colors**

Mix a bluish shadow color for the cat's coat with Titanium White, Ultramarine Blue and Burnt Sienna. First, define the nose and muzzle using a no. 3 round and a mixture created with a small portion of the bluish shadow color and Cadmium Orange, Burnt Sienna and Burnt Umber. Then, paint the shadowed areas with the bluish shadow color and a no. 7 round, using brushstrokes that follow the hair pattern. For smaller areas, such as the cat's face, use a no. 3 round. When dry, add another coat for good coverage.

Mix a ginger color for the coat with Titanium White, Raw Sienna and Cadmium Orange. Paint with a no. 3 round.

STEP 3: **Paint the Outline and Begin Detailing the Coat**

Paint the white highlighted outline of the cat with Titanium White and a no. 3 round, following the contours with your brush. Use a separate no. 3 round with the neighboring color to blend where the white meets the other color.

For the warm shadow color in the cat's coat, mix Titanium White, Ultramarine Blue, Burnt Umber and Burnt Sienna. Paint with a no. 3 round, using parallel strokes that follow the hair pattern. Blend the edges with a separate no. 3 round and the bluish shadow color.

STEP 4: **Add Detail to the Cat**

Mix a pink color for the nose and inside the ears with Titanium White, Scarlet Red, Cadmium Orange and Burnt Umber. Paint with a no. 1 round. Paint the highlighted outline of the ears and top of the head with Titanium White and a no. 1 round. Use separate no. 1 rounds to blend the white with the adjacent black and ginger.

Mix a yellowish eye color with Titanium White, Yellow Oxide, Ultramarine Blue and a touch of Cadmium Orange. Paint with a no. 1 round. Reestablish the pupils and adjust the eye shape as needed with a no. 1 round and the black.

With a no. 1 round and Titanium White, add fur detail to the face. For detail in the black fur areas, use a no. 1 round to mix some of bluish shadow color with the black on your palette. Paint strokes sparingly over the black fur. Reestablish any places that become too light with the black and a no. 1 round.

Tone down and soften the warm shadow fur detail using a no. 1 round and the bluish shadow color.

STEP 5: **Add Detail to the Fur and Fence Post**

Use a no. 1 round and Titanium White to add fur detail to the tail, the shadowed areas of the coat and around the cat's outline. Correct the outer contours as needed with a separate no. 1 round and the dark green background color. Tone down any white brushstrokes that are too prominent with a no. 3 round and some of the bluish shadow color.

Darken the shadow between the front legs and under the feet with a no. 1 round and some of the black mixed with some of the bluish shadow color.

Add detail to the fence post by painting roughly vertical cracks with a no. 3 round and the black. Add lighter tones with a no. 3 round and some of the bluish shadow color, using the same vertical strokes. Use a semi-drybrush technique with a no. 3 round to tone down and add detail with a grayish color made from the black and bluish shadow colors.

" At this point, I painted another layer of the dark green over the background for even coverage."

TIP

To achieve control of your brush when painting the whiskers, first dip it in the paint, then press down so the brush is flat (not pointed). Rest your hand on the dry surface of the painting, then paint the whiskers.

Hazel
Acrylic on Gessobord
12" x 9" (30cm x 23cm)

STEP 6: **Add Finishing Details**

Paint detail in the black part of the tail with a no. 1 round and a bit of the bluish shadow color mixed with Burnt Umber. Blend with a separate no. 1 round and the black, using the same brush and color to "fuzz" the edges of the tail.

Use a no. 1 round and a small amount of Burnt Umber thinned with water to paint a circular wash around the pupils in the eyes, blending the edges to avoid a sharp line. Paint horizontal, slightly curved arcs for highlights in the eyes with a no. 1 round and the bluish shadow color. Reestablish the pupils as needed.

Paint a thin wash of Burnt Umber with a no. 3 round over the cat's nose and the ginger-colored fur on the head.

Paint the whiskers with a no. 0 round. Use the bluish shadow color for the whiskers on the right side of the face (overlapping the background) and for above the eyes. Use Titanium White for the whiskers on the opposite side of the face. Paint with curving, light-pressured strokes.

If any whiskers come out too thick or stand out too much, use a separate no. 0 round to correct them with the color beneath the whiskers.

"To add some variety to the dark green background, I painted a lighter value green in selected areas behind the cat. I made a lighter green with some of the dark green mixed with Cadmium Yellow Light, Cadmium Orange, Titanium White and Ultramarine Blue. Using a drybrush technique, I painted dabbing, semicircular strokes with a no. 10 shader, then used a separate no. 10 shader to blend the two greens.

"I integrated the cat with the background using a very thin wash of the dark green over the bluish shadow areas of the coat. I used a no. 3 round to intersperse quick, light strokes. In some cases, the green was too prominent, so I toned those areas down with a no. 3 round and some of the surrounding bluish shadow color.

"To give the fence post its realistic look, I painted in the roughly vertical cracks with a no. 3 round and the black paint mixture. I added the lighter tones with a no. 3 round and some of the bluish shadow color, using the same vertical strokes. I used a semi-drybrush technique with a no. 3 round to tone down and add detail with a grayish color mixed with the black and bluish shadow color."

KITTEN

Painting Animal Friends

 Payne's
Gray

 black

Titanium
White

 light pink

Raw
Sienna

 blue eye color

Yellow
Oxide

 gray mixture

Burnt
Umber

warm white

Ultramarine
Blue

 tail tip color

Burnt
Sienna

 gray-brown
detail color

Cadmium
Red
Medium

 darker
shadows

Cadmium
Yellow Light

 darkened eye
color

REFERENCE

One day, while in a field on the back part of our farm, I heard a faint mewing. I followed the sound and eventually came upon this tiny kitten, all by herself in the grass. I took her home and named her Peanut.

BRUSHES

Nos. 3, 5 and
7 rounds

STEP 1: Establish the Form and the Dark Values

With a pencil, lightly draw the kitten onto your panel, using a kneaded eraser to make corrections. Thin Payne's Gray with water, then paint the main lines, lights and darks of the kitten with a no. 5 round. Switch to a no. 3 round for the eyes, nose and mouth.

Mix the black for the kitten with Burnt Umber and Ultramarine Blue. Paint with a no. 7 round, following the hair pattern. Use a no. 3 round to paint the outline of the eyes and the pupils.

Cats   29

STEP 2: **Paint the Middle Values**

For the shadow on the white fur, create a gray mixture of Titanium White, Ultramarine Blue and a small amount of Raw Sienna. Paint with a no. 7 round, following the hair pattern with parallel strokes.

Mix a light pink color for the nose and inside the ears with Titanium White, Cadmium Red Medium, Yellow Oxide and a touch of Raw Sienna. Paint with a no. 7 round. Mix a darker pink for the nostrils, mouth and around the eyes by adding a little more Raw Sienna, Cadmium Red Medium and a touch of Burnt Umber. Paint with a no. 3 round.

Mix the blue eye color with Titanium White, Ultramarine Blue and a small amount of Burnt Umber. Paint with a no. 3 round, correcting the eye shape as needed.

STEP 3: **Paint the Light Values**

Mix a warm white for the highlighted parts of the kitten with Titanium White and a touch of Cadmium Yellow Light. Paint with a no. 7 round, following the hair pattern. Switch to a no. 3 round for the muzzle and ears. For the slightly darker tail tip, mix a portion of the warm white and a bit of the gray from STEP 2.

STEP 4: **Add Detail**

Mix a gray-brown detail color for the shadowed parts of the coat. Take a portion of the gray from STEP 2 and mix in some Ultramarine Blue and Burnt Umber. Lightly paint the detail with a no. 5 round, then blend and soften with a separate no. 5 round and the adjacent color—the gray or black. Use no. 3 round for smaller detail, such as the muzzle.

Darken the nose and inside the ears with the darker pink and a no. 3 round, blending with a separate no. 3 round and the light pink.

Paint hairs overlapping the black parts of the kitten with a no. 3 round and the gray. With a small amount of paint and light, feathery strokes, follow the fur pattern.

STEP 5: **Refine and Add More Detail**

With a no. 3 round and the gray-brown from STEP 4, drybrush parallel strokes to soften the hairline along the kitten's back, stroking into and overlapping the black area.

Continue to paint hairs overlapping the black areas with a no. 3 round and the gray. Soften, darken or correct as needed with a no. 3 round and black. Use black to paint fuzzy hair along the outline of the tail and the black forehead patches, with curved strokes overlapping the neighboring color.

For darker shadows around the eyes and muzzle, mix a bit of the gray shadow color with black and paint with a no. 3 round. Blend with a separate no. 3 round and the gray.

Paint tufts of hair from the head and chest with a no. 3 round and the warm white from STEP 3.

Peanut
Acrylic on Gessobord
8" x 10" (20cm x 25cm)

TIP

If, while you are applying it, a glaze appears too heavy, immediately use your finger to rub the surface in a circular motion. This will ensure that the glaze will not dry before you can spread it out.

STEP 6: Paint the Finishing Details

Paint the fuzzy white hair at the outline of the ears and inside the ears with a no. 3 round and the warm white.

Mix a little of the blue eye color with some black, then use a no. 3 round to darken the blue part of the eye under the top lid, shading down into the blue. Use the same color to soften the black line around the eyes where it meets the blue. Paint small highlights in the eyes with the gray and a no. 3 round.

Warm up the shadowed areas with a very thin glaze of Raw Sienna. Using a no. 5 round, first dip the brush into the glaze, then blot quickly on a paper towel. Apply the glaze with quick, light strokes that follow the hair pattern.

Paint the whiskers, both above the eyes and around the muzzle, with a no. 3 round and the warm white. Paint thin, light strokes, with just enough water so the paint flows. Make corrections with a no. 3 round and the neighboring color.

Domestic Longhair

Painting Animal Friends

REFERENCE

One night I came home and found a young, fluffy-haired cat on our back porch, hungry and asking for help. We fed her and, of course, she stayed. She grew into a plump, not-too-bright but sweet cat with a plumed tail, named Marcie.

STEP 1: **Establish the Form**

With a pencil, lightly draw the kitten onto your panel, using a kneaded eraser to make corrections. Use Payne's Gray thinned with water to establish the form, with a no. 1 round for the facial features and a no. 5 round for the rest of the cat.

Mix a dark color for the cat's coat with Ultramarine Blue, Burnt Sienna and Burnt Umber. Paint the lines around the eyes and the pupils with a no. 1 round. Paint the dark parts of the cat's coat with a no. 7 round, with strokes that follow the hair pattern.

For the pink shadow under the chin, mix Titanium White, Scarlet Red and Burnt Sienna. Paint this area with a no. 1 round.

PAINT COLORS

 Payne's Gray

 Burnt Umber

 Burnt Sienna

 Ultramarine Blue

 Scarlet Red

Titanium White

 Raw Sienna

 Cadmium Yellow Light

 Yellow Oxide

MIXTURES

 dark color for cat's coat

 pink shadow color

 buff

 pinkish color

 blue-gray shadow color

 green

 warm white

 warm shadow color

 shadows under toes

eye highlight color

BRUSHES

Nos. 1, 2, 3, 4, 5 and 7 rounds

STEP 2: **Paint the Middle Values**

Mix the buff color for the cat's fur with Titanium White, Raw Sienna and Burnt Umber. Paint with a no. 7 round.

Paint the shadowed parts of the nose and mouth with a no. 1 round and the dark color from STEP 1. Mix a pinkish color for the nose, mouth and inside the ears with Titanium White, Scarlet Red and Raw Sienna. Paint the nose and mouth with a no. 1 round, then blend with the dark color. Paint inside the ears with a no. 3 round.

STEP 3: **Paint Shadows and Fur Detail**

Paint the cat's front legs and forehead with the buff color and the dark color using a fresh no. 5 round for each mixture.

Mix the blue-gray shadow color for the cat's fur with Titanium White, Ultramarine Blue and a touch of Burnt Umber. Paint the cat's fur with a no. 4 round, using strokes that follow the hair pattern. Use a no. 1 round for painting around the eyes and facial details.

Begin to add detail and to integrate the dark and light colored fur. Add enough water to the dark color so the paint flows, then paint the details with a no. 4 round. In areas where the detail is more muted, use a lighter touch and less paint.

Mix a green for the eye with Cadmium Yellow Light, Ultramarine Blue and a touch of Burnt Umber. Paint with a no. 1 round. Reestablish the pupils and eye shape with the dark color and a no. 1 round.

> **TIP**
>
> To keep the eye from following the edges of objects, tone them down where they run off your painting. The toned-down edges will help the viewer to focus on the subject.

STEP 4: **Add More Detail to the Cat's Fur**

Mix a warm white for the cat's fur with Titanium White and a touch of Yellow Oxide. Paint with a no. 4 round. Blend the edges where the white meets the other colors with feathery strokes. Switch to a no. 1 round for the facial detail.

Use a no. 3 round and the blue-gray shadow color to add more detail to the dark parts of the coat. To a portion of the buff mixture, add some Raw Sienna and Burnt Sienna. With a no. 3 round, define the warm shadow under the chin. Then, detail the dark parts of the coat. Blend these areas with a separate no. 3 round and the dark color.

Paint shadows under the toes with some of the blue-gray shadow color mixed with Burnt Umber.

STEP 5: **Paint the Final Details**

Round out the cat's right cheek with a no. 3 round and the warm white. If you need to, reestablish the mouth. Use a no. 1 round and the warm white to reinforce the outlines of the ears.

Mix a highlight color for the eyes with a small amount of the warm white and a touch of the blue-gray shadow color. Paint the highlights in small, curved arcs with a no. 1 round. Use a separate no. 1 round and the green to blend and reinforce the eye's shape.

Paint the whiskers with a no. 1 round and the warm white, using long, curved, sweeping strokes.

Define the cat's toes by adding some of the blue-gray shadow color with a no. 2 round. Use a separate no. 2 round and the warm white to blend. Darken the shadows under the paws with a no. 1 round and the dark color, then tone down by drybrushing with the blue-gray shadow color and a no. 2 round.

Marcie
Acrylic on Gessobord
12" x 9" (30cm x 23cm)

SIAMESE

PAINT COLORS

Burnt Umber

Ultramarine Blue

Raw Sienna

Titanium White

Yellow Oxide

MIXTURES

dark brown

buff

blue eyes

gray

shadow line on the cat's neck

slightly more shadowed part

highlight for dark brown fur

fur detail around eyes

dusty bluish color

white part of the eye

bluish highlight

whiskers

REFERENCE

I have always thought that Siamese cats were beautiful with their dark masks and sapphire blue eyes. This cat's name is Sassy.

STEP 1: **Establish the Form and Dark Values**

With your pencil, lightly sketch the cat onto the panel, using a kneaded eraser to lighten lines or make corrections. With Burnt Umber thinned with water and a no. 3 round, paint the eyes and nose, then use a no. 5 round for the broader areas.

Mix a dark brown for the cat's face and ears with Burnt Umber and Ultramarine Blue. Paint with a no. 5 round, switching to a no. 3 round around the eyes and nose. Use brushstrokes that follow the hair pattern. As the first layer of paint dries, add another coat for a good, dark coverage.

BRUSHES

Nos. 1, 3, 4 and 5 rounds

No. 8 shader

STEP 2: **Paint the Middle Values**

Mix the buff color for the cat's coat with Titanium White and Raw Sienna. Paint strokes that follow the hair growth pattern with a no. 5 round.

For the blue eyes, mix Ultramarine Blue and Titanium White. Paint with a no. 3 round. Use a separate no. 3 round and the dark brown from STEP 1 to reinforce the eye's shape as needed.

Mix a gray for the nose and muzzle with Titanium White, Ultramarine Blue and a small amount of Burnt Umber. Paint with a no. 3 round.

STEP 3: **Begin Adding Detail**

Begin to add detail to the cat's fur with a no. 5 round and the dark brown from STEP 1. Mix the dark brown with enough water to make it flow smoothly.

Mix some of the gray from STEP 2 with some Titanium White. Use this color and a no. 5 round to paint a shadow line on the cat's neck with parallel strokes.

STEP 4: **Paint the Light Values and Add Detail**

Mix a cream color for the fur with Titanium White and a small amount of Raw Sienna. For the slightly more shadowed part, mix Titanium White with small amounts of Raw Sienna and Ultramarine Blue. Follow the pattern of the fur with parallel brushstrokes and a no. 5 round. Switch to a no. 3 round for smaller details. With a separate no. 3 round and the buff from STEP 2, blend where the two colors meet. Use a no. 5 round to paint the light colored fur against the background.

Painting Animal Friends

Sassy
Acrylic on Gessobord
8" x 10" (20cm x 25cm)

STEP 5: **Add the Finishing Details**

To highlight the dark brown fur, mix Burnt Umber, Ultramarine Blue and a small amount of Titanium White. Paint with a no. 3 round, using parallel strokes that follow the fur pattern. Also use this color to detail the cat's irises; paint small, parallel strokes that follow the curvature of the eye with a no. 3 round. Soften these lines with a no. 3 round and the blue eye color. Add detail to the nose with the same color and brush.

Take a portion of the buff color and mix it with a little Burnt Umber, then detail the fur detail around the eyes, on the muzzle and on the ears with a no. 3 round. Use a separate no. 3 round to lightly drybrush the dark brown along the edges, blending to create a soft look. Use the same brush and color to soften the edges of the cat's mask where it meets the buff.

For the shadows on the lighter fur, create a dusty bluish color. Mix Titanium White with touches of Raw Sienna and Ultramarine Blue. Paint with a no. 5 round. Mix a bit of Titanium White with a touch of Ultramarine Blue to paint highlights in the eyes. Mix this bluish highlight color with a touch of Burnt Umber to paint the white part of the left eye. Paint with a no. 3 round, blending the edges with a separate no. 3 round and the neighboring color.

To soften the ears against the background, use a no. 3 round and the dark brown to paint small, thin strokes around the edges of the ears. Use just enough water so the paint flows. Mix a color for the whiskers with a portion of the cream and a touch of Ultramarine Blue. With a no. 3 round and just enough water for the paint to flow, lightly paint slightly curved strokes.

2

Dogs

Our family loves dogs. I'm happy that we live on a farm, because it has allowed us to give homes to quite a few dogs who were down on their luck and really needed our help. All of them have repaid us with their grateful, affectionate and intelligent companionship.

One of my favorite rescue stories is about Sasha, a mostly German Shepherd dog I spotted at the corner of two rural roads in Texas. She was obviously waiting for whoever had abandoned her there to return. She would not approach me or anyone else who tried to coax her, and would run into the road if approached, but always returned to the same spot. All I could do was put food out for her. This went on for several days, and I had concluded that I would never be able to gain this dog's trust. I decided to take a photo of her and send it to the local newspaper, hoping they would publish it and her owner would come back for her. When I arrived at the crossroads, she was sitting with her ears pricked, looking at me intently. As I crouched to take the picture, Sasha got up, as if she had already made up her mind, and hesitantly walked toward me. I stretched out my arm, talking in a soothing voice as she came closer. Shyly, she approached and eventually leaned against my arm and licked my nose! She looked overwhelmed by her decision to trust me and a little unsure, but happy as she jumped into my car. I rode home with her front feet in my lap. Over the past seven years, Sasha has proven to be a wonderful dog. She has nine canine companions—two Dalmatians, a white shepherd, two hounds, and several mixed breed dogs—all with their own rescue stories to tell. As my husband Tim says, "We just can't resist a fuzzy face!"

Webster
Acrylic on Gessobord
10" x 8" (25cm x 20cm)

DALMATIAN

Painting Animal Friends

Payne's Gray

black

Burnt Umber

pinkish brown

Ultramarine Blue

bluish shadow color

Titanium White

warm white

Cadmium Red Medium

dark brown eye color

Yellow Oxide

light blue highlight

Cadmium Yellow Light

pink

darker shadows

BRUSHES

Nos. 1, 3 and 5 rounds

REFERENCE

Our dalmatian, Katie, is the subject of this demonstration. Dalmatians are unusual dogs, both in appearance and in behavior. They're alert and active during the day, but once they are bedded down for the night, they do not like to be disturbed! They like their routines and are almost catlike in their adherence to them. Dalmatians are so different from other dogs, that, as a family joke, we refer to them as aliens.

STEP 1: Establish the Form and the Dark Values

Draw the dog lightly in pencil onto the panel. Use Payne's Gray thinned with water and a no. 3 round to paint the main lines and values. Use a no. 5 round for the broad areas of shadow on the dog.

Mix the black for the ear and collar with Burnt Umber and Ultramarine Blue (you'll add the dalmation's spots later). Paint with a no. 3 round.

Mix a pinkish brown for inside the hind leg with Titanium White, Cadmium Red Medium, Burnt Umber and Ultramarine Blue. Paint with no. 3 round, using parallel strokes, feathering the edge so that it will be easier to blend into the next color.

STEP 2: **Paint the Middle Values**

Mix the bluish shadow color for the dog's coat with Titanium White, Ultramarine Blue and Burnt Umber. Paint with a no. 3 round, with smooth strokes.

STEP 3: **Paint the Light Values and Add the First Few Spots**

Mix a warm white for the dalmatian's coat with Titanium White and a touch of Cadmium Yellow Light. Paint with a no. 5 round, using smooth strokes that follow the contours. With a separate no. 5 round and the bluish shadow color from STEP 2, blend where the colors meet. Switch to a no. 3 round for details. Soften and integrate the bluish shadow areas by drybrushing the warm white over them with a no. 5 round.

Blend the pinkish brown shadow on the inside of the hind leg with the bluish shadow color, using a no. 3 round.

Mix a bit of the bluish shadow color with the black, then use a no. 1 round to paint the buckle on the collar.

Looking at the reference photo for placement, start painting the dalmatian's spots. Use a no. 3 round and the black from STEP 1.

STEP 4: **Paint the Finishing Details**

Finish painting the spots, then use a no. 1 round and the bluish shadow color to paint highlights on the nose and collar. Paint the white markings on the ear with the warm white and a no. 1 round.

Mix a dark brown eye color with Burnt Umber and a bit of the black. Paint the eye with a no. 1 round. Apply a light blue highlight (Titanium White, Ultramarine Blue and a touch of Yellow Oxide) with a no. 1 round.

For the muzzle, neck, chest, legs and around the eye, mix a pink from Titanium White, Cadmium Red Medium and Yellow Oxide. Paint the areas sparingly with a no. 1 round, keeping the amount of paint and your brushstrokes light. Blend with a separate no. 3 round and the warm white from STEP 3.

Add a few more shaded areas in the white part of the coat with the bluish shadow color and a no. 3 round. Mix a bit of the bluish shadow color with a bit of the black to paint darker shadows on the legs, chest and neck.

Katie
Acrylic on Gessobord
10" x 8" (25cm x 20cm)

Mixed Breed

Painting Animal Friends

PAINT
COLORS   MIXTURES

Payne's   warm black
Gray

Ultramarine bluish color
Blue

Burnt   reddish brown
Sienna

warm white

Titanium
White

light eye detail

Burnt
Umber

basic
Cadmium   background
Orange   color

Raw Sienna   tan for floor

Yellow   dog's shadow
Oxide

BRUSHES

Nos. 1, 3 and
5 rounds
No. 8 shader

REFERENCE

A few years ago I found Laika, a border collie mix, looking lost and alone near our front gate. Since we could not find an owner, we kept her. She was a very sweet and intelligent dog. Two years later, Laika disappeared from our farm. We never found her, and I will always miss her.

STEP 1: **Establish the Form and the Dark Values**

Draw the dog lightly in pencil, using a kneaded eraser to make corrections or lighten dark lines. Use Payne's Gray thinned with water and a no. 5 round to paint the main lines and indicate the shadowed areas of the dog. For smaller details, switch to a no. 3 round.

Mix a warm black for the dog's coat with Ultramarine Blue and Burnt Sienna. Paint with a no. 5 round, switching to a no. 1 round for details. You will need to apply at least three coats, allowing the layers to dry in between for a good, dark coverage.

STEP 2: **Paint the Middle Values**

Mix the bluish color for the light reflections on the black coat with Titanium White, Ultramarine Blue and a small amount of Burnt Sienna. Paint with a no. 5 round, adding a second coat as the first layer dries. Switch to a no. 3 round for details.

Mix a reddish brown for the warm coat reflections, the collar and the eyes with Burnt Sienna, Burnt Umber, Cadmium Orange and smaller amounts of Ultramarine Blue and Titanium White. Paint the coat reflections with a no. 3 round, using parallel strokes that follow the hair pattern, then paint the collar and the eyes.

STEP 3: **Paint the Light Values and Add Details**

Mix a warm white for the dog's muzzle, chest and toes with Titanium White and touches of Yellow Oxide and Raw Sienna. Paint with a no. 3 round.

Take a portion of the warm black from STEP 1 and transfer it to a dry wax paper palette. (This will make the paint more opaque.) With a no. 3 round, paint small, parallel strokes that follow the hair pattern over the bluish and reddish brown areas. Use just enough water so that the paint flows easily, and a light pressure on the brush. Add a few dark hairs to the white chest marking, then paint strokes from the edges of the mark into the white to integrate. Use a no. 1 round and the warm black to reestablish the shape of the eyes. Add detail to the nose, muzzle and feet.

Painting Animal Friends

"The subdued background I chose to use in this painting is a classic choice for portraits because it complements the subject without distracting from it. To begin, I mixed a basic background color with Titanium White, Raw Sienna and Burnt Sienna. I made a modified version of this mixture—Titanium White, Raw Sienna, Ultramarine Blue, Burnt Umber and a bit of Burnt Sienna—for the dog's shadow on the wall and floor. To paint the dog's shadow, I used a no. 5 round around the dog's outline and a no. 8 shader for the broader areas, dabbing with semi-circular strokes. With a fresh no. 8 shader, I painted the wall behind the dog with the basic background color, blending the edges where it met the shadow. Next, I darkened the upper corners with a no. 8 shader and the shadow color, blending with the basic background color where needed.

"For the floor, I mixed together a tan color from Titanium White and Raw Sienna. I painted sweeping, horizontal brushstrokes with a no. 8 shader, switching to a no. 3 round around the dog's feet."

STEP 4: **Paint the Finishing Details**

Add bluish reflection detail to the coat with a no. 3 round and the color from STEP 2, softening and blending with the warm black as needed. Add reddish brown detail with a no. 3 round, again using the warm black to soften. For areas where the reddish detail is more muted—the tail, neck and chest—mix a bit of the bluish color with a portion of the reddish brown.

Add highlights to the collar with some of the warm white from STEP 3 and a no. 3 round. Use the same color and brush to define the white toes and the white tail tip.

Add lighter detail to the eyes with a mixture of Titanium White, Yellow Oxide and Raw Sienna. Paint curved arcs in the lower parts of the eyes with a no. 1 round.

Laika
Acrylic on Gessobord
10" x 8" (25cm x 20cm)

Jack Russell Terrier Puppy

Painting Animal Friends

PAINT COLORS

Burnt Umber

Burnt Sienna

Ultramarine Blue

Cadmium Orange

Yellow Oxide

Permanent Hooker's Green

Cadmium Yellow Light

Titanium White

MIXTURES

dark brown shadow color

warm black

dark green color

red color for puppy's coat

bluish shadow color

darker bluish shadow color

buff highlight color

warm white

red/warm white mixture

highlight color

whisker color

lighter green

basic grass color

REFERENCE

Baby dogs are endearing animals with their short noses, floppy ears, soft fur and innocent eyes. I saw this Jack Russell terrier puppy at a horse show having a picnic in the grass with his owners.

"*I mixed the dark green color for the puppy's shadow in the grass with Permanent Hooker's Green, Burnt Umber and smaller amounts of Cadmium Orange and Ultramarine Blue. I painted with a no. 5 round, with parallel strokes the same length as the blades of grass.*"

STEP 1: Establish the Form and the Dark Values

Lightly sketch the puppy onto the panel. Use Burnt Umber thinned with water and a no. 5 round to paint the main lines and dark areas.

Mix the dark brown shadow color for the puppy with Burnt Umber, Burnt Sienna and Ultramarine Blue. With a no. 5 round, paint parallel strokes that follow the hair pattern.

Mix the warm black for the eyes, nose and area around the eyes and muzzle with Burnt Umber and Ultramarine Blue. Paint with a no. 5 round, switching to a no. 3 round for the eyes.

BRUSHES

No. 1, 3, 5 and 7 rounds

No. 8 shader

STEP 2: **Paint the Middle Values**

Mix the red color for the puppy's coat with Burnt Sienna, Cadmium Orange and Yellow Oxide. Paint with a no. 5 round, using strokes that follow the hair pattern.

Mix the bluish shadow color for the shaded parts of the white areas of the coat with Titanium White, Ultramarine Blue and Burnt Umber. Paint with a no. 5 round. Mix a darker version of this color for the muzzle and around the eyes with more Ultramarine Blue and Burnt Umber. Paint with a no. 3 round.

STEP 3: **Add Detail to the Puppy**

Using separate no. 3 rounds for the dark brown and warm black from STEP 1, and the red color from STEP 2, blend where these colors meet. Use fine, parallel strokes, alternating between the colors. Use the warm black to sharpen the dark parts of the ears. Add detail to the puppy's red spots with the dark brown and a no. 3 round.

TIP

Soften the shadow between the head and the large red spot by thinly glazing the area with the red coat color and a no. 3 round. If you need to blend this, use the bluish shadow color.

"I mixed the basic grass color with Permanent Hooker's Green, Cadmium Orange, Burnt Umber, Yellow Oxide and Titanium White. I painted with a no. 8 shader, with dabbing strokes, switching to a no. 5 round for around the puppy's outline."

STEP 4: **Add the Lighter Values**

Mix a buff highlight color for the red parts of the puppy's coat with Titanium White, Yellow Oxide and Cadmium Orange. Paint with a no. 3 round, with strokes following the hair pattern. Blend with a separate no. 3 round and the red coat color from STEP 2.

Add some lighter hairs to the red spots with the buff and a no. 3 round, using a small amount of paint and light, feathery strokes. Blend with a separate no. 3 round and the red.

Use a no. 3 round to paint some of the bluish shadow color from STEP 2 around the edge of the white marking on the face with small, parallel strokes.

Mix a warm white for the coat with Titanium White and a touch of Cadmium Yellow Light. Paint with a no. 7 round, using dabbing strokes to cover the broad areas. Overlap the edges of the dark areas with thin, slightly curved, parallel strokes, to give the look of hairs.

"I painted blades of grass with the dark green color from STEP 2 and a no. 5 round. I used sweeping strokes with just enough water so the paint would flow easily. I created a few areas of shadow by painting several parallel strokes adjacent to each other. As I transitioned to the background, I used a little more water to make the color lighter in value, and made my strokes thinner and shorter."

STEP 5: **Detail the Puppy**

With the bluish shadow color and a no. 3 round, detail the white parts of the coat. Use thin, light-pressured strokes. Blend and soften with the warm white and a fresh brush.

Using a no. 3 round and the bluish shadow color, blend the outline of the nose against the muzzle and add detail. Use the warm black to detail the muzzle, blending with the bluish shadow color.

Mix a small portion of the red with a bit of the warm white. Paint hair detail on the ears and head with light-pressured strokes and a no. 3 round. Blend with the buff color. Use the red/warm white mixture to soften the edges of the red spots against the white coat, blending with warm white. Use the red with a no. 1 round to blend the edges of the black around the eyes and muzzle with feathery strokes.

Paint highlights in the eyes with the bluish shadow color and a no. 1 round.

TIP

In the midst of working on a painting, it is a good idea to occasionally hold it up to a mirror. Any distortions that have crept in (e.g., one eye larger than the other or a wrong angle) will immediately pop out at you. Sometimes, I stand in front of the mirror with my paints and make corrections. You can hold your reference photo and the painting side by side and look at them in the mirror. The mirror gives you a fresh perspective, almost as if you have put the painting against the wall for a couple of weeks.

STEP 6: **Paint the Finishing Details**

Mix a small amount of the buff color from STEP 4 with Titanium White. Use a no. 3 round to paint highlights along the top of the head and ears. Soften the dark edge of the right ear against the white coat by painting a line of the red along the edge with a no. 3 round. Blend with warm white and a separate no. 3 round.

Blend the edges of the red spots against the white coat with separate no. 3 rounds for the red and warm white.

Paint the whiskers with a no. 1 round and the bluish shadow color mixed with a bit of Titanium White. Paint fine, curving strokes. Tone down or correct with the neighboring color.

Little Jack
Acrylic on Gessobord
8" x 10" (20cm x 25cm)

" *I mixed a lighter green for the grass by mixing a portion of the basic grass color with Titanium White, Cadmium Yellow Light and Cadmium Orange. I painted some lighter blades of grass with a no. 3 round. I integrated the puppy with the grass by adding a few strokes of the red coat color mixed with a bit of the buff color.*

"I helped integrate the puppy with his background by painting a thin glaze of the dark green from STEP 2 and water over the left side, the tail, and the right side beneath the muzzle. I used a no. 5 round to paint light, feathery strokes that follow the hair pattern."

Yorkshire Terrier

REFERENCE

Sindy belonged to Laurie, a nice lady from France whom I met at an art show in Long Island. She commissioned me to paint a portrait of her little dog.

PAINT COLORS

 Payne's Gray

 Burnt Umber

 Ultramarine Blue

Titanium White

 Raw Sienna

 Cadmium Orange

Yellow Oxide

MIXTURES

 dark steel gray

 black

 dark brown

 middle value blue-gray

 middle value tan

 eye color

 light tan

 highlight gray

 head highlight

 long hair tufts from ears

 detail color

bright highlights on the head

BRUSHES

Nos. 3 and 5 round

STEP 1: **Establish the Form and the Dark Values**

With your pencil, lightly sketch the dog onto the panel, using a kneaded eraser to make corrections or lighten lines as needed. Use Payne's Gray thinned with water and a no. 3 round to paint the main lines of the dog.

Mix a dark steel gray for the gray fur's shadowed areas with Burnt Umber, Ultramarine Blue and a small amount of Titanium White. Paint with a no. 5 round.

Mix the black for the nose, mouth and around the eyes with Burnt Umber and Ultramarine Blue, painting with a no. 3 round.

Mix a dark brown for the tan fur's shadowed areas with Burnt Umber, Raw Sienna and a small amount of Ultramarine Blue. Paint with a no. 5 round. Add another coat for good coverage.

STEP 2: **Paint the Middle Value Colors**

Mix a middle value blue-gray for the gray part of the coat with Titanium White, Ultramarine Blue and Burnt Umber. Paint with a no. 5 round, following the fur pattern with long, smooth brushstrokes. Dab a highlight on the nose with a no. 3 round.

Mix a middle value for the tan part of the coat with Raw Sienna, Cadmium Orange and a small amount of Burnt Umber. Paint with a no. 5 round.

Mix the eye color with Burnt Umber and Raw Sienna. Paint with a no. 3 round. With the dark brown from STEP 1 and a no. 3 round, paint the pupils and reinforce the dark outlines around the eyes.

STEP 3: **Paint the Light Values**

Mix the light tan color for the dog's coat with Titanium White and a small amount of Yellow Oxide. Use a no. 3 round to paint smooth, flowing strokes. Use just enough water so the paint flows.

Mix the highlight color for the chair and for the gray parts of the dog's coat with Titanium White and a small amount of Ultramarine Blue. Paint the dog's highlights with a no. 3 round.

> **TIP**
>
> If your colors begin to dry out on the dry wax paper palette, lightly spray them with water from a spray bottle.

STEP 4: **Add Detail to the Tan Parts of the Coat**

With a no. 3 round, glaze the light tan fur with the middle value tan from STEP 2. To reestablish the highlights on the head, mix a portion of the light tan from STEP 3 with Titanium White and paint with a no. 3 round. Refine the fur using two no. 3 rounds, one for the light tan and one for the middle value tan. Paint fine lines with the middle value tan, blending with the light tan, and then vice versa. Use enough water for the paint to flow easily.

Detail the dark brown shadow areas of the ears, head and chest with a no. 3 round and the middle value tan. Use a no. 3 round to blend and reestablish the darks as needed, then add some darker detail to the dog's muzzle with fine, parallel strokes. In the shadowed areas, add a few fine lines of the dark brown.

Paint some long hair tufts from the ears with a no. 3 round and a mixture of the light tan and a bit of the middle value tan, softening the tips of the tufts.

STEP 5: **Add the Final Details**

Sindy
Acrylic on Gessobord
8" x 10" (20cm x 25cm)

With a no. 3 round, take a bit of the middle value blue-gray from STEP 2 and mix it with a bit of the dark steel gray from STEP 1. Use this color to add detail to the darkest parts of the coat with flowing strokes. Use a separate no. 3 round and the dark steel gray to detail the blue-gray fur of the coat and the tan fur of the hind legs. Paint fine strokes following the fur's pattern. Blend and soften with a separate no. 3 round and the neighboring color.

Paint locks of hair from the legs and hindquarters, using separate no. 3 rounds for the middle value gray, the dark value gray and a new tan color (a mixture of the dark and middle value tans). Add some lighter locks with the new tan mixture.

Detail the feet with separate no. 3 rounds for the dark brown and middle value tan.

Mix the eye highlight color with a small amount of the blue-gray and Titanium White. First, reduce the size of the lock of hair falling across with right eye using the eye color and a no. 3 round. Then, paint the highlights in small, curved arcs.

Paint highlights on the nose with a no. 3 round and the blue-gray. Blend with a separate no. 3 round and the black from STEP 1.

Brighten the highlights on the head with a mixture of Titanium White and a touch of Cadmium Yellow Light. Paint with a no. 3 round, using a separate no. 3 round with the middle value tan to blend and soften.

GOLDEN RETRIEVER

Painting Animal Friends

REFERENCE

Golden retrievers are a popular breed because they seem to embody what a lot of people think of as the ideal family dog: they are good natured, playful and affectionate. Webster, a dog whose portrait I painted for his owners, was no exception.

STEP 1: **Establish the Form and the Dark Values**

Draw the dog lightly in pencil, using a kneaded eraser to lighten any dark lines or make corrections. Use Burnt Umber thinned with water and a no. 4 round to establish the form.

Mix Burnt Umber and Ultramarine Blue for the black parts of the dog—nose and jowls. Paint with a no. 3 round. Mix Burnt Umber, Burnt Sienna and Ultramarine Blue for the shadowed parts of the dog's coat. Paint with a no. 5 round, using strokes that follow the hair pattern. For the darkest shadows, apply more than one coat of paint after the first layer is dry.

PAINT COLORS   MIXTURES

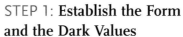
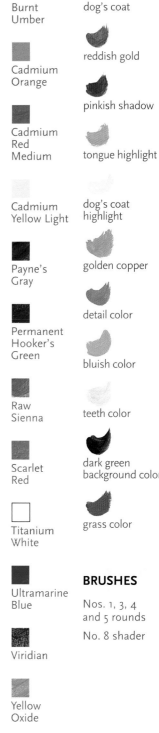

Burnt Sienna — black

Burnt Umber — shadowed dog's coat

Cadmium Orange — reddish gold

Cadmium Red Medium — pinkish shadow

Cadmium Yellow Light — tongue highlight

Payne's Gray — dog's coat highlight

Permanent Hooker's Green — golden copper

Raw Sienna — detail color

Scarlet Red — bluish color

Titanium White — teeth color

Ultramarine Blue — dark green background color

Viridian — grass color

Yellow Oxide

BRUSHES

Nos. 1, 3, 4 and 5 rounds
No. 8 shader

STEP 2: **Paint the Middle Value Colors**

Mix the reddish gold color for the retriever's coat with Raw Sienna and Burnt Sienna. Paint with a no. 4 round. Paint thinly enough so the white panel shows through so it is not opaque, with strokes that follow the hair pattern.

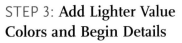

" I mixed the dark green background color with Viridian, Cadmium Orange and Burnt Umber. I used dabbing strokes with a no. 8 shader, switching to a no. 4 round for around the dog's outline. For the foreground grass, I painted sweeping strokes with the no. 8 shader."

STEP 3: **Add Lighter Value Colors and Begin Details**

Mix a pinkish shadow color for the tongue with Scarlet Red, Burnt Sienna and a small amount of Ultramarine Blue. Paint with a no. 3 round. For the tongue's highlight color, mix Titanium White, Scarlet Red and Yellow Oxide. Paint with a no. 3 round.

Mix a highlight color for the dog's coat with Titanium White and a small amount of Yellow Oxide. Transfer a portion of this color to a dry sheet of wax palette paper then use a no. 3 round to paint.

Transfer a portion of the shadow color from STEP 1 to the dry paper. Begin to integrate the dark shadows in the dog's coat with a no. 3 round, painting strokes in the direction of hair growth. Start your strokes from the shadows and overlap the lighter areas.

" I darkened the background by adding another layer of the dark green color using the same brushes."

Webster
Acrylic on Gessobord
10" x 8" (25cm x 20cm)

STEP 4: **Add the Finishing Details**

Mix a golden copper color for integrating the dog's coat with Titanium White, Raw Sienna, Yellow Oxide and small amounts of Cadmium Orange and Burnt Sienna. With a no. 3 round, paint strokes that follow the hair pattern, from the lighter parts of the coat overlapping the darker areas. For details in the darker parts of the coat, take a portion of this color and add more Cadmium Orange and Burnt Sienna. Use a separate no. 3 round and the shadow color from STEP 1 to soften and integrate. Use a no. 3 round and the darker golden copper to add some detail to the highlighted parts of the dog's coat.

For the bluish areas of the nose and jowls, mix Ultramarine Blue, Burnt Umber and Titanium White. Paint with a no. 1 round.

Use a no. 1 round to mix a small amount of Titanium White with touches of Ultramarine Blue and Burnt Umber, then paint the teeth.

" I mixed a portion of the dark green background color with Titanium White and Cadmium Orange. Then, I used this color to paint some blades of grass around the dog with a no. 3 round, using sweeping, curved strokes."

3

Horses

Ever since I was a small child, I have loved horses. My grandfather worked at Calumet Farm in Kentucky and introduced me to my first horses when I was three years old. I can still remember seeing the horses looking out of their stalls. I grew up in New Jersey where there was no place to keep a horse, so I had to content myself with drawing pictures of them and reading horse stories. My favorite book was *Black Beauty.*

When I was in my late thirties, my husband, son and I moved to the family farm in Kentucky, and one of the first things we did was acquire some horses. Getting to know these beautiful animals has been one of the high points of my life. We now have seven of them—two Arabians, two Belgian draft horses, a paint horse and two small Shetland ponies. I love watching them—whether they are galloping through a field or just quietly grazing and swishing their tails. They are definitely some of my favorite subjects to paint.

Sturdy Paint
Acrylic on Gessobord
10" x 8" (25cm x 20cm)

THOROUGHBRED

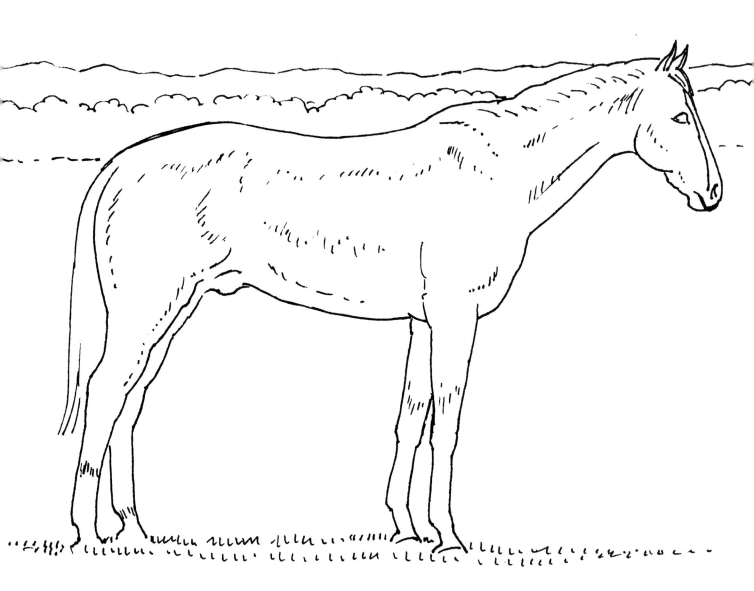

Painting Animal Friends

REFERENCE

Vasari was a handsome thoroughbred hunter-jumper horse. I was fortunate to be able to travel to California to sketch and photograph Vasari. His owner commissioned me to do three paintings of him—a head study, an informal pose and a conformation pose. This illustration serves as a study for the third painting.

STEP 1: Establish the Form and the Darker Values

Draw the horse's outline lightly in pencil, using a kneaded eraser to lighten any lines that become too dark. With a no. 4 round and Burnt Umber thinned with water, paint the darker areas.

For the black parts of the horse—the mane, tail and lower legs—mix Burnt Umber, Ultramarine Blue and a small amount of Burnt Sienna. Paint with a no. 4 round, dipping the brush first in water, then blotting on a paper towel before dipping it into the paint. To achieve a good dark covering, paint three to four coats, letting the paint dry in between layers.

For the coat's dark brown, mix Burnt Sienna and Ultramarine Blue. Paint with a no. 8 shader for the broad areas, switching to a no. 4 round for the details. Feather the edges to avoid a sharp line when you apply the next color.

 darkest brown

 Ultramarine Blue

 middle value brown

 Burnt Sienna

bluish color

Titanium White

 lightest highlight

Cadmium Orange

 darker highlight

Yellow Oxide

 highlight in the eye

Raw Sienna

 shadow for white socks

warm white

BRUSHES

Nos. 3, 4 and 6 rounds

Nos. 8 and 10 shader

STEP 2: **Paint the Middle Value Colors**

Mix a middle value brown for the horse's coat with Burnt Sienna and Cadmium Orange. Paint with a no. 4 round. In areas that will be highlighted, use paint thinned with quite a bit if water. Use brushstrokes that follow the horse's body contours. Mix the bluish color for the shadowed areas of the horse's white sock and stocking, the hooves, the highlights on the top of the tail and the upper edge of the hind leg with Titanium White, Ultramarine Blue and Burnt Sienna. Paint with a no. 4 round.

STEP 3: **Blend the Dark and Middle Values**

Using separate no. 4 rounds and the color mixtures for the dark and the middle value browns, blend the edges where these colors meet. Blend wet-into-wet. When this is dry, overlap the edges with parallel brushstrokes. Paint details on the broad dark areas with strokes of the middle value brown. Add more layers to strengthen the middle value brown. Use a no. 4 round and a wash of Ultramarine Blue thinned with water to tone down and darken the horse's coat.

STEP 4: **Refining Details and Painting Highlights**

With a no. 4 round and the dark value brown, refine the edge lines of the horse's lower neck, cheek, chin, blaze and belly. Strengthen the darks on the legs, tail and mane with a no. 3 round and the black. Mix the lightest highlight color with Titanium White and small amounts of Cadmium Orange and Yellow Oxide. Paint the highlights on the back and rump with a no. 4 round, using light-pressured, parallel strokes that follow the body contours. With Cadmium Orange and Yellow Oxide, mix a darker highlight color for the head, belly, legs and lower rump. Paint with a no. 4 round, using parallel strokes. Use this darker highlight color to soften and blend the edges of the brighter highlights on the back and rump, alternating with a separate no. 4 round and the lighter highlight color. Then, blend the edges of the highlights with a no. 4 round and the middle value brown from STEP 2, using the same technique.

Vasari
Acrylic on
Gessobord
8" x 10"
(20cm x 25cm)

STEP 5: **Add the Finishing Details**

Use no. 1 rounds to finish the details of the head and the legs. Refine the shape of the eye, ears, mouth, and back legs with the color mixtures from the previous steps. Mix a warm white with the Titanium White and a touch of Yellow Oxide to paint the blaze. Soften the edge with the darker highlight color. Paint a highlight in the eye as a small curved arc with some of the bluish shadow color mixed with a bit of Burnt Umber, then blend the edge of the highlight with the eye color and a separate brush. Define the shadow area of the white socks with the bluish shadow color mixed with a little Burnt Umber. Use a different brush with Titanium White mixed with a little of the bluish color to blend. Tone down the rump highlight with a wash of Raw Sienna and water using a no. 6 round. Tone down the white sock on the near hind leg by making a wash with the bluish shadow color and applying with a no. 3 round.

TIP

If your paint is too soupy on the Sta-Wet palette, transfer a portion of your colors to a sheet from a wax paper palette. The paint will quickly start to dry to a thicker consistency.

SHETLAND PONY

MIXTURES

black

dark brown
eye color

middle
value gray

warm brown

light blue-gray

warm yellow

warm white

shadow
detail straw

lighter
barn wood

background
highlight color

BRUSHES

Nos. 1, 3, 5
and 7 rounds

PAINT COLORS

Payne's
Gray

Burnt
Umber

Ultramarine
Blue

Titanium
White

Raw
Sienna

Yellow
Oxide

REFERENCE

We bought Moonlight about fifteen years ago, not knowing that we were getting two for the price of one! Several months later, Moonlight gave birth to a tiny foal we named Epona. Both mother and daughter have been our pets ever since.

> "*I* used the black mixture and a no. 5 round to paint the dark spaces between the boards with sketchy, vertical strokes. Next, I added the pony's shadow in the straw with dabbing strokes."

STEP 1: Establish the Form and the Dark Values

Lightly draw the pony onto the panel with your pencil, using a kneaded eraser for corrections. With Payne's Gray thinned with water and a no. 5 round, paint the main lines and values, switching to a no. 3 round for details.

Mix the black for the pony's coat with Burnt Umber and Ultramarine Blue. Paint with a no. 5 round, switching to a no. 3 round for details. For the dark brown eye color, mix more Burnt Umber into a portion of the black.

STEP 2: **Paint the Middle Values**

Mix a middle value blue-gray for the pony's nose, halter, highlight under the left eye, lower legs and the line of the belly with Titanium White, Ultramarine Blue and Burnt Umber. Paint with a no. 3 round.

A mixture of Burnt Umber, Titanium White and Raw Sienna works well on the nose and around the pony's eyes.

"For the barn wood, I used the same color that I did for the nose and around the pony's eyes—Burnt Umber, Titanium White and Raw Sienna. I painted with a no. 7 round, dabbing vertical brushstrokes (horizontal for the baseboard). I reestablished the dark spaces between the boards with a no. 3 round and black."

STEP 3: **Paint Light Values**

Mix a light blue-gray with Titanium White and small amounts of Ultramarine Blue and Burnt Umber. Paint this color on the belly, legs, back, mane and tail with a no. 5 round to indicate shadows and shape.

Mix a warm yellow with Titanium White, Yellow Oxide and Raw Sienna. With a no. 3 round, paint some long strokes on the mane and tail.

Mix a warm white from Titanium White and a touch of Yellow Oxide. Paint with a no. 7 round, with dabbing strokes on the body and long, flowing strokes on the mane and tail.

STEP 4: **Blend the Colors and Add Detail**

Using separate no. 3 rounds for the black from STEP 1 and the middle value blue-gray from STEP 2, begin detailing the pony's head. Blend with the neighboring color. Add detail to the forelock with both colors, using flowing strokes and a small amount of paint.

With the warm brown from STEP 2, drybrush details in the black part of the hindquarters, neck and chest. Use a separate brush to add detail with the middle value gray, blending with a no. 5 round and the black.

Add detail to the warm white part of the body, mane and tail with the light blue-gray from STEP 3 and a no. 5 round. With a no. 3 round, paint some of the warm brown from above onto the halter, letting some of the middle value blue-gray remain.

"*Here, I took a portion of the barn wood color and added some Raw Sienna. With this color and a no. 3 round, I painted shadow detail in the straw with basically horizontal, slightly curved strokes that varied in direction.*

"*At this point, I began detailing the barn. For this, I mixed together a lighter color for the barn wood with Titanium White, Raw Sienna and Yellow Oxide. With a fairly dry no. 5 round, I followed the wood grain with light-pressured brushstrokes. I used a fresh no. 5 round and black to detail the dark wood grain.*"

TIP

The middle value blue-gray may appear too bright in some areas. Tone it down by mixing in a little black.

STEP 5: Paint the Finishing Details

Add some detail to the mane and tail. Use a no. 3 round and Titanium White to soften and tone down the blue shadow line at the crest of the mane, then add hair tufts from the mane, tail and legs.

Tone some of the middle value grays and light blue gray areas by selectively painting some of the warm yellow onto the belly, back, legs, mane and tail. Using a no. 5 round, drybrush the color on the body with long strokes, and short, light strokes on the mane and tail. Tone down and blend with a separate no. 5 round and the light blue-gray from STEP 3.

Use a no. 3 round to tone down the nose with a wash of black and water. Refine this area with the middle value blue-gray and a no. 3 round.

For the highlight in the eye, paint a small curved arc with a no. 1 round and the middle value gray. Make corrections with a fresh no. 1 round and the dark brown eye color.

Moonlight
Acrylic on Gessobord
8" x 10" (20cm x 25cm)

" *I* decided to tone down the dark lines between the wood boards. They were too strong, leading the eye away from the pony and out of the painting. To tone them down, I used a no. 7 round to drybrush some of the barn wood color over the dark lines so that they became lighter towards the top.

"Once I was satisfied with that, I moved on to the straw. With a no. 7 round, I laid a glaze of the warm yellow over the straw. Next, I darkened the pony's shadow on the floor with black and a no. 5 round, adding a few dark strokes to the straw with a thinned black. I mixed a bit of Titanium White with a portion of the warm yellow to paint some highlights.

"With no. 3 rounds for the middle value blue-gray and the warm white, I worked to make the pony's feet show a bit more through the straw. I used another no. 3 round and the warm yellow to overlap the hooves with a few blades of straw."

Draft Horse

Painting Animal Friends

PAINT COLORS

Burnt Umber

Burnt Sienna

Ultramarine Blue

Cadmium Orange

Yellow Oxide

Titanium White

MIXTURES

dark shadow color

black

red

bluish shadow color

blonde

warm gray

shadowed hooves

highlighted hooves

shadowed blaze

detail color

darker detail

details in the dark shadows

eye highlight

warm white

highlight for horse's coat

BRUSHES

Nos. 1, 3 and 5 round

No. 8 shader

REFERENCE

Nelly is one of our Belgian draft horses. She is a big, strong mare with a beautiful flowing mane and tail. Nelly is smart, too: when a horse fly is bothering her, she will run toward the nearest person, and then quickly position herself so the selected person can swat the pesky fly.

STEP 1: Establish the Form and the Dark Values

With your pencil, lightly draw the horse onto the panel, using a kneaded eraser for corrections or to lighten lines that come out too dark. Use Burnt Umber thinned with water and a no. 5 round to paint the main lines and shadow areas.

Mix Burnt Umber, Burnt Sienna and Ultramarine Blue for the dark shadow color. Paint with a no. 5 round for the darkest shadow areas, adding another layer after the first coat is dry. Switch to a no. 3 round for smaller areas.

Mix the black for the nostrils and muzzle with Ultramarine Blue and Burnt Umber. Paint with a no. 3 round.

STEP 2: **Paint the Middle Values**

Mix the red coat color with Burnt Sienna, Cadmium Orange and a small amount of Titanium White. Paint with a no. 5 round, using a no. 8 shader for the broader areas. Use dabbing strokes that follow the horse's contours.

Mix the bluish shadow color for the white parts of the lower legs and around the nostrils and mouth with Titanium White, Ultramarine Blue and a small amount of Burnt Sienna. Paint with a no. 3 round.

STEP 3: **Paint the Lighter Value Colors**

Mix a blonde color for the mane, nose and lower front legs with Titanium White, a small amount of Yellow Oxide and a bit of Cadmium Orange. Paint with a no. 3 round, using flowing strokes for the mane.

Mix a color for the shadowed parts of the hoofs. First, create a warm gray with Titanium White, Burnt Umber and Ultramarine Blue. Take a small portion of this warm gray and add more Burnt Umber and Ultramarine Blue. Paint the shadows with a no. 3 round. For the highlighted parts of the hoofs, mix a bit of the warm gray with some of the blonde.

For the shadowed part of the blaze, mix a bit of the bluish shadow color from STEP 2 with some Titanium White and a touch of Burnt Sienna. Paint with a no. 3 round.

STEP 4: **Add Detail**

Reestablish the eye's shape with a no. 1 round and the dark shadow color. Mix a small amount of this color from STEP 1 with some Burnt Sienna. Use a no. 5 round to detail the horse's coat with parallel strokes that follow the fur pattern. Use a no. 3 round with the red coat color from STEP 2 to soften the edges.

With your palette knife, transfer a small amount of the red to a clean spot on your palette, then make a glaze with water. Paint a thin wash over the blond mane, muzzle and lower legs to make these areas glow in the late afternoon light.

Use a no. 3 round to mix some of the dark shadow color with a bit of the bluish shadow color. Use this to paint darker detail on the hoofs and lower legs, using a no. 3 round to blend into the neighboring color. Mix some of the red with Burnt Sienna for the details in the dark shadows of the horse's coat, and paint with a no. 3 round.

Mix a highlight for the eye by mixing a bit of the bluish shadow color with a touch of Burnt Sienna. Use a no. 1 round to paint the curved arc. With a no. 1 round, tone down the bluish highlights around the nostrils and chin with a thin glaze of the dark shadow color. Use a separate no. 1 round and the bluish color to soften.

STEP 5: **Add the Finishing Details**

Paint the white, highlighted part of the horse's white face marking with Titanium White mixed with a touch of Yellow Oxide and a no. 3 round. On a dry palette, mix a highlight color for the horse's coat with Cadmium Orange, Yellow Oxide and a small amount of Titanium White. Use a no. 3 round to drybrush the highlights with small, parallel strokes.

Add more detail to the mane and tail with separate no. 3 rounds for the highlight color, red coat color and dark shadow color. Add some highlights to the nose and lower legs with a no. 3 round and Titanium White mixed with a small amount of Yellow Oxide.

Nelly
Acrylic on Gessobord
10" x 8" (25cm x 20cm)

FOAL

REFERENCE

One misty morning on a horse farm in central Kentucky, I met this handsome colt. Even at this young age, you can already see the regal stance of the thoroughbred.

STEP 1: **Establish the Form and Add the Dark Values**

Draw the foal lightly in pencil onto your panel, using a kneaded eraser for any corrections. With a no. 3 round and Burnt Umber thinned with water, paint the main lines of the foal, indicating the light and dark areas.

Mix Burnt Umber and Ultramarine Blue for the black for the ears, eyes, muzzle and darker body shadows. Paint with a no. 3 round.

Mix Burnt Umber, Burnt Sienna, Raw Sienna and a small amount of Ultramarine Blue for the dark brown areas of shadow. Paint with a no. 5 round, using a no. 3 round for the smaller details. Use a no. 3 round to paint black accents over the dark brown on the lower legs, chest, etc.

PAINT COLORS   MIXTURES

 Burnt Umber

  black

 Ultramarine Blue

 dark brown shadows

Burnt Sienna

 red chestnut

Raw Sienna

golden buff

Cadmium Orange

bluish shadow color

Titanium White

warm white

Yellow Oxide

highlight color

Cadmium Yellow Light

eye highlight

BRUSHES

Nos. 1, 3 and 5 rounds

STEP 2: **Paint the Middle and Lighter Values**

Mix a red chestnut for the foal's coat with Burnt Sienna, Cadmium Orange and Titanium White. Paint with a no. 5 round, following the hair pattern with parallel strokes.

Mix a golden buff color for the lighter parts of the foal's coat with Titanium White, Yellow Oxide and Cadmium Orange. Paint with a no. 5 round.

Mix the bluish shadow color for the coat with Titanium White, Ultramarine Blue and Burnt Sienna. Use a no. 5 round for the legs and a no. 3 round for the halter, muzzle and eyelids.

Mix the warm white for the legs and the white star on the forehead with a portion of the golden buff color mixed with more Titanium White. Paint with a no. 3 round.

STEP 3: **Add Detail to the Foal**

Blend the foal's coat using separate no. 3 rounds for the red chestnut and the golden buff. Blend where the two colors meet, using a small amount of paint and light-pressured strokes. Use the same technique to blend the foal's other colors—dark brown and red chestnut, and red chestnut and bluish shadow colors. In some areas, such as the upper part of the left hind leg, blend by painting thin parallel strokes of red chestnut over the bluish shadow color. Use these same brushes and colors to add detail to the foal.

Paint the tail with dark brown and a no. 3 round, with slightly curved strokes. Use a separate no. 3 round and the bluish shadow color to paint a subtle highlight on the top of the tail, softening the edges.

> **TIP**
>
> Although it doesn't show in the reference photo, you can use your artist's license to paint the foal's tail. This gives the painting a more lifelike quality, as if the foal had just swished his tail.

STEP 4: **Paint the Finishing Details**

Mix a highlight color for the foal with Titanium White and a touch of Cadmium Yellow Light. Paint with a no. 3 round.

Mix a bit of Titanium White, Ultramarine Blue and a touch of Yellow Oxide with a touch of Burnt Umber. Use this mixture to paint highlights in the eyes with a no. 1 round, with small strokes.

Chestnut Colt
Acrylic on Gessobord
10" x 8" (25cm x 20cm)

TIP

To make the background look farther away than the foreground, use colors that are lighter in value and more bluish. This is called atmospheric perspective.

Paint Horse

Painting Animal Friends

PAINT COLORS

 Payne's Gray

 Raw Sienna

 Burnt Umber

 Burnt Sienna

 Ultramarine Blue

Titanium White

 Scarlet Red

 Cadmium Orange

Cadmium Yellow Light

 Yellow Oxide

MIXTURES

 dark brown

 bluish shadow color

 warm pink shadow

 red

 lighter blue shadow

 pink for the horse's nose

 eye

eye highlight

warm white

 highlight red

BRUSHES

Nos. 1, 3, 5 and 7 rounds

REFERENCE

This strikingly patterned paint mare was part of a herd of paint horses on a farm in Kentucky. I spent the whole morning sketching and photographing the horses. They have been the subjects of several of my paintings.

STEP 1: **Establish the Form and Dark Values**

Draw the horse lightly in pencil, using a kneaded eraser to make corrections or lighten lines that are too dark. With Payne's Gray thinned with water and a no. 4 round, paint the main lines and form.

Mix a dark brown for the shadowed parts of the red coat with Burnt Umber, Burnt Sienna and Ultramarine Blue. Paint with a no. 3 round. When the first layer of paint is dry, add another coat.

Mix a bluish shadow color for the white parts of the horse with Ultramarine Blue, Burnt Sienna and Titanium White. Paint with a no. 3 round.

Mix a warm pink shadow color for the nose with Titanium White, Burnt Sienna, Scarlet Red, Cadmium Orange and Burnt Umber. Paint with a no. 3 round.

STEP 2: **Paint the Middle Value Colors**

Mix the red for the horse's coat with Burnt Sienna, Cadmium Orange and Scarlet Red. Paint with a no. 5 round.

Mix the lighter blue shadow color with Titanium White, Ultramarine Blue and a small amount of Burnt Sienna. Paint with a no. 5 round.

TIP

It's okay to make changes in a painting as you go along. I decided that including the nearer trees that appear in the reference photo would have distracted from the openness of the landscape behind the horse.

STEP 3: **Paint the White Parts of the Horse and Details**

Mix the pink for the horse's nose with Titanium White, Raw Sienna, Scarlet Red and a touch of Cadmium Orange. Paint with a no. 3 round. Blend the edges where the pink meets the darker color on the nose with a no. 1 round and some of the warm pink shadow color from STEP 1.

Mix the eye color with Burnt Umber and a bit of Burnt Sienna. Paint the eyes with a no. 1 round, adding another coat when it's dry. Mix Titanium White with a touch of Ultramarine Blue for the highlight, and paint in a curved arc with a no. 1 round. Correct and blend with the dark eye color and a no. 1 round.

Mix a warm white for the white parts of the horse on a piece of dry wax paper with Titanium White and a touch of Yellow Oxide. Paint with a no. 3 round, switching to a no. 1 round for the smaller details. Use a no. 3 round with the neighboring color to correct and blend the edges. If the paint begins to dry on the wax paper, add water.

Sturdy Paint
Acrylic on Gessobord
10" x 8" (25cm x 20cm)

STEP 4: **Add Finishing Details**

Mix a highlight color for the red parts of the coat with Titanium White, Cadmium Orange, Yellow Oxide and Cadmium Yellow Light. Paint with a no. 3 round, following the contours with parallel brushstrokes. With a fresh no. 3 round, blend the red coat color with quick, light strokes. Adding the red will also warm up the highlights.

Use a no. 7 round and a wash of Burnt Umber and water to paint a shadow on the horse's belly and on the shadowed white part of the left hind leg. With a no. 3 round and the bluish shadow color, add a little more detail to the white parts of the horse's head and body. Use a small amount of paint and fine, parallel lines. Soften with a separate no. 3 round and the warm white.

TIP

At times, you will need to use your artistic license to make something stand out that blends into the background in your reference photo—for example, the right hind leg of the horse. Selectively darken the shadows and the highlights on the leg so it stands out from the front leg.

4

Cattle

I was introduced to cows on a family trip to Ideal Farms in New Jersey, where they raised dairy cattle. I remember being surprised at how big they were when I first saw them up close!

After I was married, my husband and I often walked on my husband's family farm in Kentucky, and I always enjoyed seeing the cows. There is something very peaceful about a field full of cattle, especially when it is dusk and they are settling down for the night. In the springtime, the calves are fun to watch as they scamper and play together. In the winter, I like seeing their wooly coats and their warm breath in the cold air.

Now that we have our own farm, we have our own cattle. Some of these cows we brought back from a three year stay in Texas, and others came from Kentucky, so we have a mixture of longhorn, Brahman, Hereford and Angus. Eleven of these cows have names and are permanent residents. I never tire of sketching, photographing or just observing them in their daily lives.

Classic Holstein
Acrylic on Gessobord
8" x 10" (20cm x 25cm)

CALF

Painting Animal Friends

PAINT COLORS

 Burnt Umber

 Burnt Sienna

 Ultramarine Blue

 Permanent Hooker's Green

 Cadmium Orange

☐ Titanium White

 Cadmium Red Medium

 Yellow Oxide

 Raw Sienna

 Cadmium Yellow Light

MIXTURES

 dark brown

 red coat

 pink

 gray

 buff

 bluish gray

 detail

highlight

BRUSHES

No. 1, 3 and 5 rounds

REFERENCE

Last spring, this pretty calf was born to our part-longhorn cow, Aster. We named her Astrid. Her reddish coloring and white markings make her an attractive subject to paint.

STEP 1: Establish the Form and the Dark Values

With your pencil, lightly draw the calf onto the panel, using a kneaded eraser to lighten lines or make corrections. Use Burnt Umber thinned with water and a no. 3 round to paint the main lines of the calf.

Create a dark brown for the shadows using Burnt Umber, Burnt Sienna and Ultramarine Blue. Paint the dark parts of the calf with a no. 5 round, using a no. 1 round for the eyes and nostrils. Paint with smooth strokes that follow the calf's contours. Dab the paint onto the forehead for the calf's curly hair.

STEP 2: **Paint the Middle Values**

Mix a red for the coat with Burnt Sienna, Cadmium Orange and a small amount of Titanium White. Paint with a no. 5 round, switching to a no. 3 round for smaller areas.

Mix a pinkish color for inside the ears with Cadmium Red Medium, Cadmium Orange, Burnt Sienna and a small amount of Titanium White. Paint with a no. 5 round.

Mix a gray for the nose with Titanium White, Burnt Umber and Ultramarine Blue. Paint with a no. 3 round.

STEP 3: **Paint the Light Values**

Mix a buff color for the lighter parts of the calf with Titanium White, Raw Sienna and a small amount of Cadmium Orange. Paint with a no. 3 round, using strokes that follow the hair pattern.

For the shadows in the calf's white markings, you'll need a lighter, slightly bluish gray. Mix Titanium White and small amounts of Ultramarine Blue and Yellow Oxide. Paint with a no. 3 round, using dabbing strokes.

STEP 4: **Paint Detail in the Coat**

Transfer some of the dark brown from STEP 1, some of the red from STEP 2 and some of the buff from STEP 3 to a dry wax paper palette. Use a no. 3 round and the dark brown to detail the coat with small, parallel brushstrokes that follow the hair pattern. Blend and soften with a separate no. 3 round and the red coat color. Use the same dark brown and brush to detail the buff-colored areas of the coat, then use a separate no. 3 round and the buff to blend.

Transfer a portion of the bluish gray from STEP 3 to the dry palette. Mix a color for adding detail to the white areas of the coat with the bluish gray and small amounts of the dark brown and red. Paint with a no. 3 round.

Detail the nose with the dark brown and the gray from STEP 2, using fresh no. 3 rounds for each.

TIP

When painting a portrait background—which consists of one color—you can achieve a sense of atmosphere by varying the paint thickness, letting some of the underlying panel show through in places.

STEP 5: **Add the Highlights and Finishing Details**

On the dry palette, mix the highlight color for the calf with Titanium White and a bit of Yellow Oxide. Use a no. 3 round to paint with fairly thick strokes, then blend the edges with a separate no. 3 round and the red.

Use a no. 3 round and the red to add some lighter detail to the shadowed parts of the calf—the front legs, forehead, chest, etc. Use a moderately dry brush with light-pressured strokes. Using the same technique, paint some detail in the red areas of the coat with the buff color.

Paint the highlights in the eyes in small, curved arcs, with a bit of the bluish gray and a no. 1 round. Use the same color and brush to paint highlights around the nostrils.

Astrid
Acrylic on Gessobord
10" x 8" (25cm x 20cm)

Cow's Head

Painting Animal Friends

PAINT COLORS

Payne's Gray

Burnt Umber

Ultramarine Blue

Burnt Sienna

Cadmium Orange

Raw Sienna

Titanium White

Yellow Oxide

Cadmium Yellow Light

MIXTURES

 warm black

 dark brown shadows

 reddish

 buff

 warm gray

 blending color

warm white

 light blue-gray

highlight color

 lower eyelids

 shadowed area of the belly

details over the shadowed area

blue sky color

BRUSHES

Nos. 0, 1, 3 and 4 rounds

No. 8 shader

REFERENCE

We lived in Kaufman County, Texas for several years on a small farm with five cows. When we moved back to our family farm in Kentucky, we took the cows with us. Jessamine is a big, beautiful cow with dark eyelashes, large ears and horns, all part of her Brahman heritage.

STEP 1: **Establish the Form and the Dark Values**

Draw the cow's head lightly in pencil, using your kneaded eraser to make corrections or lighten any lines that are too dark. With Payne's Gray thinned with water and a no. 3 round, establish the main lines and form. Switch to a no. 4 round for the broader areas.

Mix the warm black for the darkest areas on the face, ears and horns with Burnt Umber and Ultramarine Blue. Paint with a no. 3 round, switching to a no. 4 round for the broader areas. Mix Burnt Sienna and Ultramarine Blue for the dark brown shadows on the neck and paint with a no. 4 round.

STEP 2: **Paint the Middle Value Colors**

Mix a reddish color for the coat with Burnt Sienna and Cadmium Orange. Paint with a no. 3 round, switching to a no. 8 shader for broad areas. Use brushstrokes that follow the cow's shape. Once this dries, add another coat for good coverage.

Create a buff color for the muzzle and horns with Titanium White and Raw Sienna. Paint with a no. 4 round.

Mix the warm gray for the nose and horn detail with Titanium White, Burnt Umber and Ultramarine Blue. Paint these areas with a no. 3 round. Use the warm gray and a no. 0 round to paint under the eyes. For the chin, mix a little warm black with some of the warm gray. Paint the reflected light under the chin with a mixture of the warm gray and a little Titanium White and a no. 3 round.

STEP 3: **Begin Adding Detail**

Mix some of the warm black with some Burnt Umber. With a no. 3 round, blend where the black areas meet the reddish areas, using small strokes that overlap the edges where the two colors meet. Paint hair detail in the reddish areas, with strokes that follow the hair pattern. Make the edges of the ears fuzzy with small strokes and add detail to the nose and horns.

" *The only background I wanted for the cow's head was a cloudy sky. I started with a blue sky color, mixed from Titanium White, Ultramarine Blue and a small amount of Yellow Oxide. I mostly painted with a no. 8 shader, but switched to a no. 4 round to paint around the outline of the cow. I painted the clouds Titanium White, using a fresh no. 8 shader and blending the edges where the white met the blue while both colors were still wet.*"

> *" I finished the sky using the same brushes and colors. I simply reinforced the blue and added more clouds, blending while wet, then drybrushing the edges of the clouds."*

STEP 4: Paint the Blaze and the Coat Highlights

For the warm white of the blaze on the cow's forehead, mix Titanium White with a touch of Cadmium Yellow Light. Use a no. 4 round to paint with dabbing strokes. Overlap the edges of the blaze where it meets the reddish color with a no. 1 round, using small strokes that follow the hair pattern. To detail the white blaze, mix a light blue-gray from Titanium White with small amounts of Ultramarine Blue and Burnt Sienna. Paint with a no. 3 round, using slightly curved strokes. Blend with a separate no. 3 round and the warm white.

Mix the highlight color for the cow's coat with Titanium White, Cadmium Orange, Yellow Oxide and a small amount of Cadmium Yellow Light. Paint the highlights on the head and ears with a no. 3 round, using a small amount of paint and light-pressured strokes that follow the hair pattern. Paint small, slightly curved triangular tufts. Use a separate no. 3 round with the reddish color to soften and blend. Paint the highlights on the body using parallel brushstrokes that follow the general contours.

Reinforce the lower eyelids with a mixture of Titanium White, Ultramarine Blue and a bit of Burnt Sienna using a no. 1 round. Use a no. 3 round and the same color to paint muted highlights in the black points of the face, ears and nose. Blend the nose detail by alternately painting small strokes of the warm gray and small strokes of the buff.

Jessamine
Acrylic on Gessobord
9" x 10" (23cm x 25cm)

TIP

Make the cow's left ear stand out more by toning down the shadow of the ear on the body. Use a no. 3 round and a mixture of the highlight color and a little Burnt Sienna. Paint with light-pressured, semi-dry strokes.

STEP 5: **Add the Finishing Details**

Add some Burnt Umber and Ultramarine Blue to a bit of the reddish coat color. Paint the shadowed area of the belly using a no. 4 round, with strokes that follow the contours. Mix some of the coat's highlight color with a little Cadmium Orange and Burnt Sienna to paint a few details over the shadowed area with a no. 4 round.

Add more detail to the horns with a no. 3 round. Paint a glaze of Burnt Sienna over the horns, then add some staggered, broken lines with the warm black.

Blend the edges of the blaze using a no. 1 round and the warm white. Paint small strokes out from the edges to overlap the reddish color.

Add highlights to the eyes with two no. 1 rounds. Use the first one to paint the highlight with the light blue-gray from STEP 4. Using the second brush, quickly blend the highlight's edges with the dark eye color.

Strengthen the black ear fringes with the warm black and a no. 3 round. Soften the sharp outlines with a no. 1 round and a small amount of the reddish coat color.

HOLSTEIN

Payne's
Gray

warm black

Burnt
Umber

grayish highlight

Ultramarine
Blue

warm shadow
color

Titanium
White

pink

Raw
Sienna

bluish shadow
color

Yellow
Oxide

lighter gray

Cadmium
Red
Medium

warm white

Cadmium
Yellow Light

darker shadow
color

eye highlight

BRUSHES

Nos. 1, 3, 5
and 7 rounds

REFERENCE

This cow belongs to some neighbors of ours who run a small dairy farm. The whole family very kindly helped me get the cow into a good pose, repeatedly herding her away from a muddy puddle she wanted to wade in to cool off!

STEP 1: **Establish the Form and the Dark Values**

Draw the cow lightly in pencil. With Payne's Gray thinned with water and a no. 5 round, paint the main lines and form of the cow.

For the warm black of the cow's coat, mix Burnt Umber and Ultramarine Blue. Paint with a no. 7 round, with dabbing strokes that follow the cow's contours. As the paint dries, add more layers until the black is rich and dense.

TIP

Although the cow's tail doesn't show in the main reference photo, adding the tail gives more life to the pose, as if the cow had just flicked away a fly.

STEP 2: **Paint the Middle Values**

Mix a grayish highlight color for the black areas of the coat with Titanium White, Burnt Umber and Ultramarine Blue. Paint with a no. 5 round.

Mix a warm shadow color for the cow's chest, belly, udder, legs and tail with Titanium White, Yellow Oxide, Raw Sienna and Ultramarine Blue. Paint with a no. 5 round.

Mix a pink for the nose and udder with Titanium White, Cadmium Red Medium and Yellow Oxide. Paint with a no. 3 round.

STEP 3: **Paint the Lighter Values**

Mix a bluish shadow color for the white areas of the cow with Titanium White, a small amount of Ultramarine Blue and a touch of Burnt Umber. Paint with a no. 5 round.

Blend the grayish highlight color with the warm black of the cow's coat using separate no. 3 rounds for the two colors. Use a fairly dry brush to paint small strokes of black over the highlighted areas, then blend with the grayish color.

Drybrush more grayish highlights over the black areas.

STEP 4: **Paint the Lightest Values and Add Detail**

Mix a lighter gray highlight color with a bit of the grayish highlight color from STEP 2 and Titanium White. Paint the highlights on the head and ears with a no. 3 round.

Mix a warm white for the cow's coat with Titanium White and a touch of Cadmium Yellow Light. Paint with a no. 3 round, with small, dabbing strokes.

Mix a darker shadow color for the cow's chest, belly, udder, legs and tail with a portion of the warm shadow color from STEP 2 mixed with Burnt Umber and a small amount of the warm black from STEP 1. Paint with a no. 3 round, using a fresh no. 3 to blend it with the neighboring color.

With separate no. 3 rounds for the bluish shadow color, the warm shadow color and the warm white color, blend where those colors meet.

STEP 5: **Add the Finishing Details**

With a no. 3 round and the grayish highlight color from STEP 2 add some hair detail to the inside of the left ear. Use a no. 1 round to refine the cow's muzzle and nostrils.

With the lighter version of the warm shadow color and a no. 3 round, paint detail in the cow's white face marking and flank. Blend with a fresh no. 3 round and the warm white.

Use a no. 1 round to refine the shape of the eyes. For the highlights in the eyes, mix a bit of the grayish highlight color with a touch of the warm black from STEP 1. Paint with a no. 1 round.

Classic Holstein
Acrylic on Gessobord
8" x 10" (20cm x 25cm)

5

Barnyard Animals

One of my earliest paintings was done while I was in high school, at the request of my grandmother, who wanted a barnyard scene. The painting depicts two white ducks by a farm pond, with a cow and a red farm house in the background. I still enjoy sketching, painting and interacting with farm animals.

When I was growing up, my family raised a dozen chickens—eleven hens and a rooster. I was fascinated with the chickens and spent hours watching them. They all had names and distinct personalities, and were so tame that the hens would lay their eggs in my hand! I've gotten to know pigs on my husband's family farm, and have had pet goats and rabbits, but I would still like to know other farm animals such as sheep, donkeys, llamas, ducks and geese. So many animals—so little time! But even if I can't find the time to take care of all these animals, I can still enjoy doing paintings of them!

Happy Pig
Acrylic on Gessobord
8" x 10" (20cm x 25cm)

CHICKS

Painting Animal Friends

REFERENCE

Since I planned to paint some baby chicks for this book, I bought Casa and Blanca from a local farm supply store. I had actually been wanting to get a couple of chickens, and this was a perfect excuse! They grew rapidly and are now beautiful white chickens with red combs.

 Burnt Umber — dark brown

 Raw Sienna — red-gold

 Cadmium Orange — pink

Titanium White — accent color

 Cadmium Red Medium — blue-gray

Cadmium Yellow Light — yellow

 Ultramarine Blue — warm white

 highlight detail

 light pink

 highlights

 dark detail

 slate blue

STEP 1: Establish the Form and the Darker Values

With a pencil, lightly draw the chicks onto your panel. Use Burnt Umber thinned with water and a no. 5 round to paint the main darks and lights, switching to a no. 3 round for details.

Mix the dark brown for the eyes and the dark shadows on the feet and legs with Burnt Umber, Raw Sienna and Cadmium Red Medium. Paint with a no. 3 round.

BRUSHES

Nos. 1, 3 and 5 rounds

STEP 2: **Paint the Middle Values**

Mix a red-gold for the shadows on the chicks with Cadmium Orange, Raw Sienna and Cadmium Yellow Light. Paint with a no. 5 round, with parallel strokes following the pattern of the down.

Mix a pink for the legs, feet and beaks with Titanium White, Cadmium Orange, Cadmium Red Medium, Cadmium Yellow Light and a touch of Raw Sienna. Paint with a no. 3 round. Then, take a portion of this color and mix with Burnt Umber and Burnt Sienna. Use this color with a no. 3 round to accent the feet, legs and around the beaks.

Mix the blue-gray with Titanium White, Ultramarine Blue and a touch of Cadmium Orange. Paint this mixture on the left side with a no. 5 round.

Mix the yellow for the chicks' down with Titanium White, Cadmium Yellow Light and a touch of Raw Sienna. Paint with a no. 3 round. Begin to blend where the yellow meets the red-gold with a no. 3 round, using small, parallel strokes.

STEP 3: **Paint the Light Values and Details**

Mix a warm white for the highlighted parts of the chicks with Titanium White and a small amount of Cadmium Yellow Light. Paint with a no. 5 round, switching to a no. 3 round for details.

You'll need a detail color for the highlighted areas. For this, mix a portion of the yellow with some of the red-gold from STEP 2. Use a no. 3 round to paint parallel strokes, then blend.

Mix a light pink for the highlighted parts of the beaks, legs and feet with a portion of the pink from STEP 2 mixed with Titanium White. Paint with a no. 3 round. Add detail to the beaks, feet and legs using separate no. 3 rounds for the different colors. Add highlights with a bit of the warm white mixed with the yellow. Add dark detail to the beaks with some of the pink mixed with some of the dark brown.

Casa and Blanca
Acrylic on Gessobord
5 ¹/₂" x 8" (14cm x 20cm)

STEP 4: **Paint the Finishing Details**

Mix a slate blue for shadowing on the chicks with Titanium White, Ultramarine Blue, Burnt Umber and Raw Sienna. Paint thin, parallel strokes with a no. 3 round, then blend and soften with the adjacent color.

Transfer some of the warm white to a dry palette so the paint will become thicker. With a no. 1 round, add more detail to the downy coats.

Paint highlights in the eyes with some of the blue-gray, using a no. 1 round to paint small, curved arcs. Refine the beak of the chick on the left with a no. 3 round for each color.

Domestic Ducks

REFERENCE

One of my favorite places for photography and sketching is the Lexington Cemetery in Lexington, Kentucky. Founded in 1848, it is a beautiful place, with large, old trees, sunken gardens, flowers and secluded ponds. Many animals live there, including chipmunks, squirrels, rabbits and birds. This is where I encountered these attractive white ducks. Graceful swimmers, they seemed to glide effortlessly across the water.

STEP 1: Establish the Form and the Dark Values

Draw the ducks lightly in pencil, using your kneaded eraser for any corrections. Use Payne's Gray thinned with water and a no. 3 round to paint the basic lines, lights and darks. Use a no. 7 round for the broader areas and for the water.

Mix the dark brown for the ducks' eyes and bills with Burnt Umber and Ultramarine Blue. Paint with a no. 3 round.

For the dark shadowed parts of the feathered areas, mix a gray with Titanium White, Ultramarine Blue, Burnt Umber and a small amount of Raw Sienna. Paint with a no. 3 round, using parallel strokes.

PAINT COLORS

 Payne's Gray

 Titanium White

 Ultramarine Blue

 Burnt Umber

 Raw Sienna

 Viridian

 Cadmium Orange

 Yellow Oxide

 Cadmium Yellow Light

MIXTURES

 dark brown

gray

orange

darkened orange

 light blue

 lighter value blue

 warm white

 light orange

 dark green

 blue-green reflection

 greenish water

 lighter value detail

BRUSHES

Nos. 1, 3, 5 and 7 rounds

No. 10 shader

"I mixed the dark green for the water with Viridian, Burnt Umber, Ultramarine Blue and a small amount of Cadmium Orange. I painted with a no. 5 round, with smooth, horizontal strokes. For the broad expanses of water, I switched to a no. 10 shader, painting carefully around the ducks' outlines with a no. 5 round. When everything was dry, I added another coat.

"I mixed the blue-green reflection base color for the water from Titanium White, Viridian, Ultramarine Blue and Burnt Umber. I paint with a no. 7 round, with long, smooth, horizontal strokes.

"I created the greenish water color from Viridian, Titanium White, Ultramarine Blue and Burnt Umber. I painted these areas with a no. 7 round, using smooth strokes that followed the ripple pattern."

STEP 2: **Paint the Middle Values**

For the ducks' bills, mix an orange with Cadmium Orange, Titanium White, Yellow Oxide and a small amount of Raw Sienna. Paint with a no. 3 round. Mix a darker shadow color for the bill with the orange, Burnt Umber and more Cadmium Orange and Raw Sienna. Paint with a no. 3 round. Reestablish the line of the mouths, nostrils and darker shadows on their bill with a no. 3 round and the dark brown from STEP 1.

Mix a light blue for the ducks' shadows with Titanium White, Ultramarine Blue and small amounts of Yellow Oxide and Burnt Umber. Paint with a no. 5 round.

STEP 3: **Paint the Light Values**

With Titanium White and small amounts of Ultramarine Blue and Cadmium Yellow Light, mix an even lighter value blue for the highlighted parts of the forefront duck. Paint with a no. 5 round. Use a no. 3 round and the light blue from STEP 2 to blend where the two colors meet, using small, parallel strokes. With a separate no. 3 round and the gray from STEP 1, blend where this color meets the light blue. Begin to add some detail with the gray.

Use a no. 5 round and the light blue to add detail to the shadowed parts of the duck with light-pressured strokes.

Mix the warm white for the highlighted parts of the background duck with Titanium White and a touch of Cadmium Yellow Light. Paint the broad areas with a no. 5 round, switching to a no. 3 round for the smaller detail areas, such as the head and tail. Blend the light blue with the warm white and the gray.

Mix a highlight color for the bill of the far duck with Titanium White and touches of Cadmium Yellow Light and the orange from STEP 2. For the near duck, add a little more of the orange for a darker highlight color. Paint with no. 3 rounds, blending with the adjacent color and a separate no. 3 round.

"*With a no. 5 round and the greenish water color from STEP 3, I added ripple marks to the water with slightly curved, sweeping strokes.*"

Quacka Blanca
Acrylic on Gessobord
8" x 10" (20cm x 25cm)

TIP

For lighter value detail, mix a little of the light blue into a bit of the gray.

STEP 4: **Paint the Finishing Details**

Use no. 3 rounds to add more detail to the ducks' feathers, blending with the neighboring colors. Reestablish the shapes of the eyes as needed with a no. 1 round and the dark brown color. Paint highlights in the eyes with the lightest value blue and a no. 1 round.

"*I continued to paint ripples in the water with the greenish color and a no. 5 round. I used the light bluish color from STEP 4 and a no. 5 round to paint the ducks' reflections with horizontal strokes.*

"*I painted some orange reflections in the water from the ducks' bills with the orange bill color from STEP 3 and a no. 5 round.*"

PIG

PAINT COLORS

 Burnt Umber

 Burnt Sienna

 Ultramarine Blue

 Cadmium Orange

 Raw Sienna

Titanium White

 Yellow Oxide

 Scarlet Red

MIXTURES

 dark brown

 golden brown

basic color

pink

warm gray

 dark gray

lighter detail color

highlight color

BRUSHES

Nos. 1, 3, 5 and 7 rounds

No. 10 shader

REFERENCE

While I was driving along the back roads of Jessamine County, Kentucky, I stopped when I caught sight of this pig. She shared a field with a white goat. I was struck by her happy and contented expression, and I just had to sketch and photograph her for future reference.

STEP 1: Establish the Form and the Dark Values

With a no. 3 round and Burnt Umber thinned with water, paint the main lines and form of the pig.

Mix a dark brown with Burnt Umber, Burnt Sienna and Ultramarine Blue for the dark valued areas. Paint with a no. 5 round.

STEP 2: **Paint the Middle Values**

Mix a golden brown middle value for the pig's coat with Raw Sienna, Burnt Sienna, Burnt Umber and a small amount of Titanium White. Paint with a no. 5 round.

STEP 3: **Paint the Lighter Values**

Mix the pig's basic color with Titanium White, Raw Sienna, Cadmium Orange and Yellow Oxide. Paint with a no. 10 shader for the broad areas, using dabbing strokes. Switch to a no. 7 round for the smaller areas. Blend into the edges where it meets the neighboring color with small strokes.

Mix a pink for the pig's udder with Titanium White, Scarlet Red, Cadmium Orange and a small amount of Raw Sienna. Paint with a no. 7 round.

For the ears and snout, mix a warm gray with Titanium White, Burnt Umber and small amounts of Ultramarine Blue and Raw Sienna. Paint with a no. 3 round.

STEP 4: **Add Detail to the Pig**

Add detail to the lighter parts of the coat with the golden brown from STEP 2. Use a no. 3 round, painting small parallel strokes that follow the hair pattern. For lighter value detail, use a little more water and a lighter pressure on your brush.

To mix a dark gray for detail on the snout and ears, combine some of the dark brown from STEP 1 with Titanium White. Use a separate no. 3 round with the warm gray from STEP 3 to blend where the two colors meet. Reinforce the dark parts of the ears and snout with a no. 3 round and the dark brown. For lighter details over the broad dark areas of the pig's coat, take a portion of the basic color from STEP 3 and mix in small amounts of Yellow Oxide and Cadmium Orange. Paint with small strokes. Add some lighter colored hairs to the tail with flowing strokes.

STEP 5: **Refine the Pig's Coat**

Warm and soften the pig's coat by painting a glaze of the golden brown mixture and water over the entire body with a no. 7 round. Mix a highlight color for the pig with Titanium White and a small amount of Yellow Oxide. Use a no. 1 round to paint a smooth line around the pig's outline, then blend inward with small strokes.

Happy Pig
Acrylic on Gessobord
8" x 10" (20cm x 25cm)

ROOSTER

PAINT COLORS

Burnt Umber

Ultramarine Blue

Viridian

Burnt Sienna

Cadmium Orange

Titanium White

Yellow Oxide

Raw Sienna

Cadmium Yellow Light

Cadmium Red Medium

BRUSHES

Nos. 1, 3, 5, and 7 rounds

MIXTURES

 black

 dark green

 red-brown

 blue-green

 red

 eye color

 dark gray

 lighter gray

 reddish feather detail

 greenish feather detail

 highlight

 reddish highlight

greenish highlight

 pink

 darker comb detail

brighter highlights

REFERENCE

Last fall, on a visit to my parents' home, I went for a drive with them in the country. At a farm with a roadside stand, we stopped to look at the goats, sheep and chickens they had on display. This fine looking rooster caught my eye as he seemed to pose for his portrait.

STEP 1: Establish the Form and Dark Values

With a no. 3 round and Burnt Umber thinned with water, paint the outline and main tail feathers of the rooster. Use a no. 5 round to paint the Burnt Umber wash in the main shadow areas.

To create a black for the dark parts of the head and body, combine Burnt Umber and Ultramarine Blue. Paint with a no. 5 round. Apply a second coat when the first dries. Use a no. 3 round to paint the eye and beak.

For the green tail feathers, create a dark green mixture with Burnt Umber, Ultramarine Blue and Viridian. Paint with a no. 5 round, switching to a no. 3 round for details.

TIP

To see the dark values in your reference photo without the distraction of the feather detail, squint your eyes. These areas will pop out at you.

STEP 2: **Paint the Middle Values**

For the reddish feathers, mix a red-brown with Burnt Sienna and Cadmium Orange. Paint in smooth strokes with a no. 5 round.

Mix a blue-green for the tail feathers with Titanium White, Viridian, Ultramarine Blue and a touch of Burnt Umber. Paint with a no. 5 round, with smooth strokes following the feather contours.

Mix a red for the rooster's comb with Cadmium Red Medium and small amounts of Titanium White and Burnt Umber. Paint with a no. 3 round.

Mix the eye color with Yellow Oxide and Cadmium Orange. Paint with a no. 1 round.

STEP 3: **Paint the Dark Feather Detail**

Paint dark feather detail with a no. 3 round and the black mixture, using light-pressured strokes and a small amount of paint, with just enough water so the paint flows. Switch to a no. 1 round to reinforce the dark line around the eye, the pupil and the beak. Paint cracks in the log and darken shadowed parts of the feet with a no. 3 round.

STEP 4: **Paint Light Values and More Detail**

Mix Titanium White, Ultramarine Blue, Burnt Umber, Burnt Sienna and a touch of Raw Sienna to create a dark gray. Add more Titanium White to a portion of this for a lighter gray. Using the lighter gray and a no. 3 round, paint the beak, legs and feet. Using the black, dark gray and light gray (and a separate no. 3 round for each), blend the dark shadows on the toes into the lighter gray. Define the beak and detail the beak, feet and legs with a no. 1 round and a mixture of the black and dark gray. Use the neighboring color to make corrections to the shape if needed.

Add some reddish feather detail to the black areas of the rooster's body with some of the red-brown mixed with Cadmium Orange. Use a no. 3 round.

Mix a color for greenish feather detail on the wings, chest, back and lower neck with a portion of blue-green and a small amount of the dark green. Paint with a no. 3 round. Add a little of the red brown to the tail feathers with a fresh no. 3 round.

STEP 5: **Add Highlights and Details**

Mix a highlight color with Titanium White and a bit of Yellow Oxide. Paint highlights on the tail feathers, legs and some of the body feathers with a no. 3 round. Once you reestablish the eye color and pupil, paint a highlight in the eye with a no. 1 round and the highlight color. Use this color to paint detail in the comb, then blend with a separate no. 1 round and the red comb color.

Add lighter detail to the reddish wing feathers with some of the red-brown mixed with a bit of Yellow Oxide and Titanium White. Lightly paint parallel lines over the feathers.

Mix a highlight color for the blue-green feathers with some blue green and a touch of Titanium White and Yellow Oxide. Paint with a no. 3 round, with small, parallel strokes.

Combine a little of the red comb color and Titanium White with a touch of Yellow Oxide to create a pink for parts of the legs and feet. Paint with a no. 1 round. Mix a bit of the red comb color with Burnt Umber and use a no. 1 round to paint darker detail in the comb.

STEP 6: **Add the Finishing Touches**

Use a no. 3 round to paint a thin glaze of Burnt Sienna on the comb, beak, legs and feet.

Brighten the highlights on the legs, feet, beak and tail with a no. 3 round and Titanium White mixed with a touch of Cadmium Yellow Light.

Fancy Rooster
Acrylic on Gessobord
8" x 10" (20cm x 25cm)

INDEX

Look for these other great titles from North light Books!

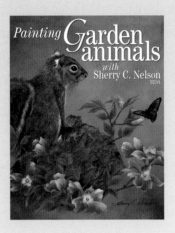

PAINTING GARDEN ANIMALS WITH SHERRY C. NELSON, MDA

Sherry C. Nelson shows you how to bring life and personality to a variety of adorable garden animals and your favorite household pets. Through clear, step-by-step demonstrations and full-color reference photos, you'll learn how to paint realistic features, such as eyes filled with awareness and fur that begs to be stroked. These ten projects depicting animals in heartwarming interactive poses will send you straight to your paints and brushes!

ISBN 1-58180-427-X; PAPERBACK ; 144 PAGES; 32591

DISCOVER THE JOY OF ACRYLIC PAINTING

Learn how to properly execute basic acrylic painting techniques—stippling, blending, glazing, masking or wet-in-wet—and get great results every time. Jacqueline Penny provides five complete step-by-step demonstrations that show you how. Practice painting a flower-covered mountainside, sand dunes and sailboats, a forest of spruce trees and ferns, a tranquil island hideaway and a mist shrouded ocean.

ISBN 1-58180-042-8; HARDCOVER; 128 PAGES; 31896-K

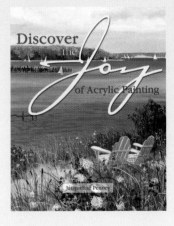

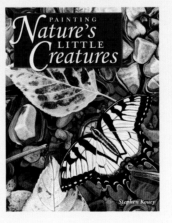

PAINTING NATURE'S LITTLE CREATURES

Subjects from ponds to trees, and even the grass beneath your feet provide a world of animal images worth capturing with your brush. Koury covers more than a dozen creatures, providing step-by-step instructions that enable you to recreate everything from translucent dragonfly wings to the damp, smoothly textured skin of frogs. It's all the instruction you need to paint nature's tiniest tenants!

ISBN 1-58180-162-9; HARDCOVER; 144 pages; 31911-K